Bone Orchard:
Reflections on Life
under Sentence of Death

Bone Orchard:
Reflections on Life
under Sentence of Death

George T. Wilkerson
& Robert Johnson

With contributions by
Sarah Bousquet
& Benjamin Feder

Cover Photo by Donald Kinney
Cover Design by Casey Chiappetta
Text Design by Charlotte Lopez-Jauffret
Text Editing by Kat Bodrie, Robert Johnson, &
Sophia Auger Madden

BleakHouse Publishing
2022

BleakHouse Publishing

Kerwin Building 254
American University
Washington, D.C. 20016

www.BleakHousePublishing.org

Robert Johnson – Editor & Publisher
Kat Bodrie – Chief Editorial & Marketing Officer
Charlotte Lopez-Jauffret – Chief Operating Officer
Benjamin Feder – Art Director

ISBN: 978-0-9961162-8-2

Printed in the United States of America

For all who believe in the inherent dignity and value of humanity. I'm sorry it took me so long to learn it myself. This book is also for those who believe in second chances, in life and hope, and that people can change — if given a chance. More importantly, this is for God, who is helping me to embody transformation.

– George T. Wilkerson

To George T. Wilkerson and all those whose lives embody dignity and hope in the midst of great adversity.

– Robert Johnson

Table of Contents

Part IV: Exit

About the Authors & Contributors
About the Artists, Editors, & Designers
Other Titles from BleakHouse Publishing

Acknowledgements

I want to thank my fellow men incarcerated on Death Row for being so open and honest about your internal experiences of this place. Thanks go to Andrew "Frost" Ramseur for our in-depth discussions, which helped to crystallize the concept of this book. Thanks to Dr. Robert Johnson, who greenlighted my proposal to use The List as the heart of this book and who contributed so much material to this collaboration. And to Kat Bodrie, my fellow poet and kindred spirit, who constantly helps me to expand my sense of self-awareness and plays a transformative role in developing my poetic aesthetics — I'm excited to see what our creativity brings into being. Thanks for your constructive feedback on the content I shared.

– George T. Wilkerson

I thank the many men and women who shared their prison experiences with me over the years, helping me to develop a sensibility that allows me to write with some limited authority about life in prison and under sentence of death.

– Robert Johnson

Gratitude also goes to the publications in which many of these pieces first appeared, in their current or altered forms:

Adore Noir – "Transubstantiation" by Robert Johnson; parts of "Haunted" by Robert Johnson were repurposed for "Lethal Rejection: Reveries and Ruminations on the Edge of Execution"

Crime, Media, Culture – "Lethal Rejection: Reveries and Ruminations on the Edge of Execution" (originally "Lethal Rejection") by Robert Johnson

Crimson Letters: Voices from Death Row (second edition) – "The Huggy Boys: Letter to My Mom, 2011" (originally "The Huggy Boys") by George T. Wilkerson

Death House Desiderata: A Hunger for Justice, Unsated – "A Single Olive" by Sarah Bousquet

Interface – "At the Zoo," "Little Sister" (originally "Oppa"), and "Talking to My Mom in Autumn, 2016" (originally "Talking to My Mom in Autumn") by George T. Wilkerson

Main Street Rag – "At the Zoo" by George T. Wilkerson

The Marshall Project – "Keep It Moving" (originally "The Implications of Trying to Kill Yourself on Death Row") and "Snakes and Thunder" (originally "Death Row's First Ever Talent Show") by George T. Wilkerson

The Prison Journalism Project – "Six Feet" (originally "And Then the Pandemic Began" and "In Prison during COVID-19") and "Talking to My Mom in Autumn, 2016" by George T. Wilkerson

St. Anthony Messenger – "The Knowledge of Good and Evil" by George T. Wilkerson

The Sun – "Fat Brown Quarters" by George T. Wilkerson

Walk in Those Shoes – "A Body is a Home" (originally "Six Cubic Feet"), "Fat Brown Quarters," and "The Knowledge of Good and Evil" by George T. Wilkerson

A Zoo Near You – "Circadian Rhythm" (originally "He Awakens"), "Coldest," "Flesh is Weak" (originally "Old Men"), "Lightbearers" (originally "Hope?"), "Lights Out" (originally "Years of Living Alone"), and "Witness" (originally "Execution Night") by Robert Johnson

Note: Much of the content of this book has appeared in various publications and in modified forms, but the authors retain full rights — so they publish with their permission.

Preface
The List: Basic Features
of Life on Death Row
by George T. Wilkerson

I created The List based on a one-question survey of my
fellow men on my pod on Death Row in North Carolina. It
describes what we believe to be basic features of what it's like
for people incarcerated with a death sentence. Some of the
features are universal to all Death Row prisoners, such as
being forced to confront one's own mortality. Other features
apply to North Carolina's Death Row but may or may not
apply to other states' Death Rows.

The features can be categorized in other ways, as there is
so much overlap — rarely can one tease out and isolate a
single feature to describe its effect. Thus, the features
generally work together in clusters of three or four, and
nearly every piece in this collection explores or illustrates
multiple features.

Different features are more salient to some prisoners
here than others. For example, the hardest part for me is
feeling abandoned and disconnected from my loved ones
whereas others can't stop ruminating on their impending
deaths. In the midst of all the pieces, readers will see my own
narrative thread as I come to terms with my death sentence.
One such thread includes the correspondence to my mom
that marks points in my journey; though the dates attached
are five years apart, it didn't happen so symmetrically. I
simply spaced them out to remind the reader that I am still
here amid the trials my fellow prisoners are struggling
through. Also, I wanted to convey certain emotional
resonances at key points throughout the book, and the
correspondence was a handy way to do that.

Readers will notice that this is a hybrid work containing
essays, poems, and letters. Some aspects of a condemned life
are better captured in a concentrated, tight little poem that's

heavily crafted. Others are better explored in analytical and philosophical prose or essays — still others in plain-spoken letters. The goal is to connect the human element to the abstract principle, that the two may combine to create a three-dimensional diorama of life on Death Row, contextualized within the metanarrative of mass incarceration in America.

Readers will find The List in the appendix, as well as a thematic index that allows them to home in on specific features from The List. This thematic approach may be helpful for classroom and small group discussions.

While much of the material is autobiographical or based on specific people, some characters are composites of several people — or a prototype of a personality common here. For example, the poem "Lunarspider, Lord of Nothing" is based on actual guys I know, but also represents a type of person: a bully used to getting his own way who finds himself suddenly powerless. In that sense, 'Cifer ("Lucifer" abbreviated) is a fictionalized character based on very real people. In the essays, I used people's real names except for in "Keep It Moving," where I changed the man's name to "Juda" to protect his identity.

The thing to remember is that the features of living under sentence of death as examined in this book are real, and their effects as described are real, whether the character is a composite or actual person.

Throughout the book, you will see that sometimes "Death Row" is capitalized, sometimes not. It depends on the medium and the formality, depending on context. Emphasis is also a factor. The point is that whether capitalized or not, it was intentional, not an oversight.

The book's objective is simply illustrative, a way to answer this question: *What makes serving time with a death sentence distinct from doing time with a release date?* Likely, The List is not exhaustive, but we believe it gives a fuller, more nuanced portrait of what living on Death Row for decades does to a human soul.

To learn more about the origins of The List, visit bleakhousepublishing.org/death-row-question

Part I:
Entry

Welcome: Letter to My Mom, 2006

by George T. Wilkerson

Dear Mom,

I don't blame you for disowning me. I hope it's okay for me to write you anyway. Today is my first day on death row, a hastily built wing affixed to the rear-end of Central Prison. The prison itself is *huge*, like a small city, with miles and miles of corridors big enough to drive a firetruck through. Hundreds of doorways. If they opened all the doors, I'd be lost; I have no idea how to leave this place. I was led by chain into it.

The hundreds of doorways throughout the prison are painted in plastic-playground colors — pastel shades of blue, marshmallow cream (soft and forgiving colors). But on the row, the doors are painted a congealed red, like an implicit threat. Other than the walls, it seems that *all* the painted surfaces on death row are red. The bunks, the railings, the steps, windowsills. Even our jumpsuits are red. Well, evidently, once issued a jumpsuit, we're stuck with it. So while they start off stiffly starched and vivid red, over time the heavy canvas material softens. I see men with threadbare knees and seats, their jumpsuits faded to shades of pink. I wonder how long they've been here. Decades, from the look of it. Most look sort of sickly. It's like the fading jumpsuits are a wearable metaphor for the eroding humanity here.

The guards took me to "diagnostics" earlier, to evaluate me. We walked so far, my feet hurt in these shower sandals they issued me. I swear, this prison's got a thousand tunnels! EXIT signs only lead you deeper inside. And each hall is segmented by pneumatic sally-port doors. A simple button-push on a control panel in a guard booth can instantly divide a half-mile long tunnel into a dozen chamber-locked compartments — to contain or isolate groups or individuals. Since I'm a death row prisoner, everywhere we went, tunnels were sealed off to ensure I had no interaction with the non-death row prisoners here. They're "on the yard," general population guys. Most have release dates. I could see them from a distance, through the Plexiglas. Some made fists; some beat their chests a couple times, then pointed their chin up — which I read as, "Hey, man, stay strong. Keep your head up." I would just nod, try to straighten my spine though my legs feel like jelly. I'm scared, Mom.

Other guys wouldn't even make eye contact with me.

Before my evaluation was done, the pretty lady who was screening me said, "You want some advice, young man? I'm not going to lie — you're in for some hard time. You came in alone, you'll leave alone. Learn to accept that. You try to make friends back there, it's going to break you, because you're going to have to watch them carried off to die. Death row doesn't have phone access right now except for one ten-minute call at Christmastime. Let's see, it's December 21st — y'all already had your calls, so it'll be next year for you. Better start writing letters, because most guys don't get visits and, like I said, no phone access."

So I'm writing you, though I know I'm not part of the family anymore. Even if you don't respond, I feel better writing you.

Death row itself is further divided into eight pods, each with twenty-four single-man cells, though we may come out into the dayroom and mingle among ourselves. I doubt I'll make friends; like the woman said, why bother?

I'm not afraid to die, Mom. Dying is the easy part. Waiting decades to be executed, with nobody to connect with — that's the scary part.

I suppose that's the point.

I love you, Mom. And I'm sorry: I've never been a good son. I hope you can forgive me one day, maybe even visit me. If not, I'd understand. I'm still going to write you for as long as I can afford the stamps, probably about three or four months. After that, I'll be completely cut off . . .

4

Your son,
George

P.S. Have you told Sara where I am? She's sixteen now. I'd hate for her to know. I hate worse the thought of my baby sister convinced that I just abandoned her — that I stopped coming to visit, sending gifts, etc. because I was an addict. Please tell her that I love her so much and that I'm sorry I broke my promise to always be there to protect her.

features from The List: banished, mortality, segregation, staff

Little Sister
by George T. Wilkerson

nine years: my whole life
i had waited for you. the final nine

months, every day was like the night
before Christmas as mom wiggled

my heart in my face. i labored
and walked holes into the waiting

room's floor, groaned
when i saw your creamy brown face

poke like taffy through the wrappings.
i was always *right there*, the one

you ran to, the one you trusted
to gently brake you when you fell

while learning to walk.
i told you corny jokes for hours

using googoo gibberish and eyebrow
esperanto; you'd make a mini O and go

into silent convulsions while patting at
my cheeks. you've always understood me.

my hand swallowed yours to help you
wield crayons' thumb-thick colors

to draw your first cartoons and conclusions
from the world around us. i was there

to ward the darkness off, and you
were a tiny flame for me to focus

my affection on. i made you
a PROMISE, whisper-stitched it

into your angel hair almost daily: *no one*
will ever hurt you as long as i am

around. i'm the no one
who broke you

by not being there — by running
after my addiction, then by catching

my death.

features from The List: banished, family, grief

The Code
by George T. Wilkerson

Maybe Death Row's Unit Manager thought he detected weakness in my polite demeanor or maybe it was just standard procedure — I still don't know — but my first day on Death Row, before sending me into the wilderness, the UM tested my readiness. With his tall, stocky build and shrewd eyes, he favored my big brother Michael. But he was not my brother; Michael knew not to test me.

I remember only the gist of his insult: "It can get pretty rough back there. If you ever need some help, if somebody is . . . bothering you . . . you can just drop me a note and—"

I held up my hand to cut him off. Instantly indignant, my spine stiff, I spoke firmly and carefully to make sure he understood.

"I do not need, or want, your help. Keep it. I will never drop you a note. I will never be one of your informants. Ever. I've always handled things myself, and if I get in a bind back there, I'll handle that too. With these."

I raised my fists to show him the scars and calluses on my knuckles. He was clearly unimpressed.

"But even if I lose," I continued, "I will not come to you."

He flipped a hand dismissively and circled his desk before sitting down.

"Alright, then," he said. "So you don't need one of my officers to walk you back there. Head down the hall, take a right, then turn left at the guard booth. That first pod is yours. You'll find your cell without my help."

As I left his office, I felt I'd just won my first victory toward establishing my reputation among people who knew nothing about me. In prison, I knew, reputation was everything.

* * *

Prison life cultivates sameness, regiments sameness, perpetuates sameness — of days, of experiences, of prisoners. On the surface, every detail the State intends to be the same *is* the same. We wear the same reddish jumpsuits every day like cartoon characters who age and wrinkle and fade to pink. Our food trays receive the same slack portions. The prison limits each man's belongings to the same six cubic feet and assigns each man a cell to store himself in.

At first, Death Row's everyday sameness numbed my eyes to nuance, blinded me to change and differences. It was a vast, featureless expanse of daily routine and bland patterns that replicated indefinitely. Prison culture — a prison within prison — is a cell that encapsulates a timeless reality, a cell that holds, in stasis, the same way of life that has dominated prisoners ever since The Beginning. Driven by the mythic convict code, prison culture clones homogenous thoughts, feelings, and behaviors as if stamped out on a cosmic assembly line.

The convict code is straightforward. Verily, verily, it says unto us:

> Thou shalt never cooperate with the police (guards), or else . . .
> Thou shalt respect thy neighbors (especially the bigger ones), or else . . .
> Thou shalt mind thine own damned business, or else . . .

Each man crafts his own version of code interpretation like knock-off brands. *Don't spread lies. Don't steal anyone's stuff. Don't get your nasty jack-grease on the gossip magazine I let you borrow.*

Some men set booby traps to create more rules. For example, the mop buckets in our block's two janitor closets are for communal use. One day, we got an extra bucket. When somebody used it to clean his cell, another prisoner jumped on him when he took it back to the closet.

"The fuck you doin' touchin' my shit?" he demanded.

He had laid claim to it, secretly. Because "ignorance of

the law is no excuse," as the courts say, a trial by fire ensued.

One argued the bucket was public property; the other said it was for private use only. And since every prisoner acts as a law unto himself — judge, jury, executioner — might makes right. The winner of a fist debate will get his rule ratified. And it'll stand until somebody stronger batters down the wall he erected.

Like denominations, men tend to clique up and reinforce each other's commandments. A man can friction-burn his shoulders trying to squeeze between all these arbitrary boundaries. He can also select which ones to respect and fight to erase the dominance of others. Only the weak must follow everybody's rules. A willingness to fight, which is a type of raw power, buys some freedom.

That was how I understood the nature of incarceration. I figured every person in prison accepted it the same way we accepted the rain: whether we liked it or agreed with it or not. To even speak against it was sacrilegious.

*   *   *

My first day on Death Row, a man from two cells down the line appeared in my doorway and introduced himself as Gary. He had gray hair combed neatly to the side. Because of its ragged edges, I suspected he had trimmed it himself — with toenail clippers. He proffered a white-paper lunch bag stuffed with snacks and tobacco.

"Here you go, young man," he said with a slight lisp. "Christmas is days away, and we just got our care packages, so I wanted to make sure you had something . . . "

For a few seconds, I stared at him, measuring. Was he trying to punk me? He was twice my age and out of shape, but still, I knew better than to accept "gifts."

But I also really, really wanted a cigarette, and it'd be days before the jail transferred my funds to my prison account.

So I thanked him, took the bag, and promised to pay him back.

10

"Nah," he said. "Merry Christmas. You don't owe me anything."

He grinned as I immediately started rolling up cigarettes.

That's when he shape-shifted. He stepped into my cell, and I froze. He glanced at me then redirected his attention to my cell like a flamboyant housing inspector, obviously assessing it against some mental checklist. He thumbed the buttons on my sink/toilet unit, squinted at my strip of window, traced his eyes along the floor cracks and corners, rubbed his palm on the wall, cocked his ear toward my whooshing air vent.

Perhaps thirty seconds passed before he back-stepped out of danger, and I breathed easily again. I tried to hide my trembling hand as I lit my cigarette. Gary pointedly avoided eye contact. He scowled.

"Man, this is one shitty-ass cell," he said. "Next time a cell comes open, you might want to see about getting moved."

My first thought was that he disliked his new neighbor and was indirectly telling me to leave. However, everything about him screamed, *Hi-dee-ho, neighbor!* My next thought was that I wouldn't want to move into a cell of a man who'd just been executed, and I was a little shocked I could request a cell-swap at all.

Gary continued. "Someone might go to lock-up. Or move to another pod. Or get off the Row — you never know. I've seen it happen lots of times. Or you might could pay somebody to swap cells with you, and y'all could ask the Unit Manager to make it official. Just something to think about."

I couldn't see how moving from one cell to another on the same block would make any difference, so I told him, "A cell's a cell, right? Hell, I'd still be in prison."

I tossed my cigarette butt in the toilet, trying to project an air of indifference, hoping he'd elaborate on what he'd seen wrong with my cell. I hated to reveal I was baffled.

He shrugged and left. It kind of pissed me off, but I couldn't blame him. A closed mouth won't get fed, and I had kept my confusion to myself. In prison, evidently, all cells

11

are *not* created equal. It was only after settling into Death Row's rigid uniformity that the anomalies popped out against prison life's static background.

*   *   *

When I first entered two-down, all I saw was the prototypical cell with its version of standard features: red-painted bunk bolted to rear wall, stainless steel sink/toilet unit, slightly knuckle-dented steel mirror that battered my reflection, fluorescent light fixture, steel slab desk/shelves protruding from wall, and a four-inch-tall, three-foot-long strip of window high up on the rear wall.

After Gary planted in me the promise of greener, grassier cells elsewhere, I arranged my toiletries on the high shelf, set my Bible on the desk, made my bed, and stepped to the door to watch our dayroom's TV — and to study my podmates by learning their patterns and status positions.

I noticed two things about my room right away. First, the radio reception was terrible. It could pick up the TV fine as the TV transmitted to our cigarette pack–sized radios from across the room, but as I dialed to a radio station, static crinkled the airwaves in between. Somebody told me to go stand on my bunk and look out my window. When I did, I saw a towering gray brick building an arm span away, blocking out the sky and interfering with incoming radio signals.

Second, because of the angle between my cell and the tinted-window guard booth across the dayroom, guards could observe every inch of my cell, including my toilet.

Over the next few days, it also became clear that several guys' exercise routines involved speed-walking countless laps around the dayroom (thirty-four equal one mile), which carried their chitter-chattering and shoe squeaking right past my doorway every thirty seconds.

And one hairy-fingered man my dad's age mistook an open door for an invitation to pop up and update people on, well, everything. He spoke to me as if I'd known him all my

12

life, referencing "Mom," "Cathy," "that sonofabitch who lied on me" — people I'd never heard of before. I might be writing a letter when I'd hear a voice talking, mid-stride, like a walker passing by. But it'd be Hairy Knuckles in my doorway, prattling away.

I tried dropping hints. I refused to respond or even to look up from my letter or book. It didn't matter. He kept right on, reminding me more and more of my dad, who was notorious for his soliloquies and hairiness.

My dad had died during my trial, and I missed him, and I felt guilty for having been a bad son. I thought it disrespectful for this man to violate my ears, but I couldn't bring myself to enforce the code on him. It'd be like trying to tell my lonely dad to shut up.

Some of us nicknamed what guys like him do as "taking someone hostage" or "kidnapping" them. He didn't talk with people; he talked *at* them.

We hostages developed signals to request rescue. If I spotted Hairy Knuckles (aka The Knuckle Dragger) pinning someone in a conversational headlock, I'd try to make eye contact with the wilting victim and then pat the top of my head. If he nodded, I'd engage the assailant with a question, and as he answered, I'd walk away slowly, towing him along, having now sacrificed myself so the other guy could disappear. But if I was the victim and nobody noticed, I would just do a distinct bird call like a desperate crow — "Ca-caw Ca-caw! Ca-caw Ca-caw!" — when a potential rescuer walked by.

At first, the talker recoiled — "What the hell?" — as a hostage negotiator swooped in to save the day. But before long, the talk-terrorists caught on. When I ca-cawed, they'd say, "Oh, screw you. I don't talk no more'n anybody else."

Otherwise, I could only escape by saying I really needed to poop and X-ing my arms above my head to signal the guard booth to close my door, or I could go take an hour-long shower and hope he'd latched onto someone else's ear by the time I finished.

I decided I needed a cell closer to the corner — either

five-, six-, seven-, or eight-down — to cut off most of the booth's line of sight into my cell. In any of those cells, I could also drape a privacy sheet across my doorway (at an angle, without the booth seeing it) to stiff-arm dayroom walkers' reckless eyeballs. If the talker came knocking, I'd claim I was pooping or napping.

If I could procure seven- or eight-down, which were on the long wall, I'd get great radio reception too since no buildings blocked the world beyond their windows. Even better, no traffic clogged the top-tier cells.

But more than a year would pass before any cells on my pod opened up.

*   *   *

The imprisoned soul has few pleasures and freedoms, so the ones it has multiply in significance and value. What to an outsider might seem ant-sized can become elephantine in prison. It's supply and demand: The supply of freedoms is scarce; the demand is immeasurable, nearly infinite. As each cell offers its own blend of freedoms and restrictions, its every feature demands a careful weighing, a reckoning.

A buddy of mine in his mid-sixties is going blind. No reading or writing letters, no TV, no books, not even faces. His radio is his last air hose to the world outside as darkness encloses him. He lived in the cell next to mine where bad radio reception barred his beloved baseball games and NPR. When a cell opened in another pod, he packed up and moved, leaving his friends behind and exposing himself to the trials and dangers that invariably come with having to re-establish himself around unfamiliar people. Though he had the weird, squinty-eyed look of an uncle your parents would never let you go camping with as a kid, he was over-the-top funny and a political savant.

I miss our rabid political debates, and I know he does too. But how can friends compare to a radio when most of your time is spent in a cell, alone — a cell that shrinks a little more every day and will continue shrinking until it's tighter

14

than skin, a darkening cell with only a radio as a straw to breathe through?

Once I had decided to move, I began obsessing over my cell's flaws. Being on the ground floor meant insects had chewed tunnels through the mortared seams between badly jointed prefab slabs that fit together like concrete box flaps. And the weather chased the insects into those tunnels. When it rained, the cracks where walls kissed floor moistened, then streamed. The walls seemed perpetually sheened in sweat, which explained why Gary had swiped his palm across it. Even dry, my cell smelled damp, mildewy, dank with earthy decay — but I think it was also because of the leaky sink/toilet unit. Supposedly, the maintenance man would change the rotten gasket or busted seal, but every couple months, and always in the night, it would leak. Sometimes, I'd climb out of bed at two a.m., bleary-eyed and bloated with piss, and as I stumbled half asleep to the toilet, my feet would splash in a small puddle of toilet juice.

Meanwhile, the ants were sneaky critters. They didn't skitter across my floor as did the weird roach-like insects with crab pincers on their rears, nor did they rappel down my walls like the brown recluses. I'd react to spiders and crab-roaches like there were panthers in my cell. I'd hop up, heart racing, land in my ninja stance, snatch a wad of paper towels, and pounce with a primal scream laced with terror, revulsion, and victory.

But the ants at least made an effort to hide. They attacked only the food stored in the very back of the shelf attached beneath my bunk. Since I had stocked up on cases of ramen soups, stacks of Little Debbie cakes, and bags of chips, it took me weeks to munch my way to those rear-most items. One day, I grabbed a white-icing honey bun and noticed it had thousands of black sprinkles all over it. When I realized an army of ants had somehow gotten in, committing suicide by sugar, I almost ate the honey bun — and them — as revenge. A finger-thick line of ants connected another of my cakes to a pinhole in the floor, like a living power cord running straight into the earth to supply their colony. I plugged the hole with a wad of paper towels, then poured sudsy mop water down their throats.

The top-tier cells had no creepy infestations other than their human residents, and their ceilings weren't also the floor of the cell above them, harboring exercise junkies. Mine hopped around all day, his every step beating against a muffled bass drum that rumbled like distant thunder trembling down my walls and into my nerves. With the convict code in mind, I asked myself, *Is it disrespectful for him to make all that friggin' racket over my head? Since he was here first, does he have the right of way? Do I think I can go up there and rewrite some rules?*

I was never good at talking problems out. Talking gave the other person time to break my nose while I ran my mouth. If I went to talk and it started to get heated or he crept too close, I would make sure I threw the first punch. I didn't usually bother saying anything unless I was ready to fight, and some guys automatically take any verbal confrontation as a threat. Thus, even if I had no intention of fighting, I needed to be ready in case this guy was not the talking type. I didn't think it was really worth fighting for, but I also knew my patience quickly wore thin once I got it in my head that I was being wronged.

Of course, the man above me was huge, a powerlifter. That decided it for me: I wouldn't do any talking or fighting. I'd be patient. It's interesting how my unwillingness to risk a beating changed my interpretation of the code's commands: The man in the cell above me was not disrespecting me; I was just being twitchy. His size helped me see I was the one being intrusive and inconsiderate.

Besides, I comforted myself, *you won't be in this cell much longer.* Believing that, having that bit of hope, made it more tolerable.

*   *   *

About six months before my trial — before landing on Death Row — I completed a one-year stint in solitary confinement, or "the hole." I then transferred to a pretrial detainee unit at Central Prison called Safekeeping.

Many of my podmates there were facing serious charges like me, and some of them were veterans at doing time, hard men who could help me trade in my self-titled "gangsta" persona for the applicable convict currency. I fell in with them, constantly sought their opinions, and generally acted as their disciple. These men had established reputations from their previous incarcerations, and I was very conscious of their ability to confer status.

One day, we discovered that Kurt, fortyish and who looked like a much heavier, taller, bearded version of Hitler, had informed officers of a minor illicit activity. The indigent men (i.e., even poorer than the rest of us) received ten postage stamps per month from the prison, and since they seldom enjoyed snacks from commissary, they'd trade their precious few stamps for food. The guys with the food got those stamps at twenty-five percent off, so everybody benefited.

Now, we'd lost that. The prison started giving indigent guys credits that only they could use — because of Kurt.

I looked to the veteran cons to decide how we'd handle his treachery. Would we beat him up, then force him to move to another pod? Just beat him up? Force him to pay a fine — and beat him up?

They told me they'd handle it. During deliberations, nobody was to speak to Kurt. He was invisible to us. I was anxious because I figured he would ask the guards to relocate him before we could retaliate. I was also eager to elevate my status. I hoped I'd be nominated to punish him.

Lock-in came that night and still no decision. The next morning, the old cons were playing poker as usual, and Kurt was there, sitting at his usual spot at the table, laughing and joking around with them. He wore this smug, triumphant grin when he saw me. Evidently, I'd been out-maneuvered. I looked around the pod, and nothing was amiss. Everybody was back at their usual routines, heedless of the injustice unfolding at the card table.

Are they testing me? I wondered.

I flew into a righteous rage. I ran to the table, snatched the cards, and flung them into the air, sending them flapping everywhere like a flock of startled birds.

"What the hell y'all doing being cool with this snitch?!" I screamed. "He can't make money with us anymore! He can't break bread with us! We ain't even supposed to let him sleep in our pod!"

I tried to yank Kurt away from our table. He was docile, but the other men broke my grip and tried to calm me down. This wasn't a test; they were serious.

"Chill out, li'l bruh," they said. "That ain't how we carry it here."

"What do you mean that ain't how y'all carry it? That's the rules!"

"Whose rules? Who made those rules? Some other old convicts none of us have ever met! We didn't make those rules, and we sure as hell didn't agree to them. You just comin' off the streets and tryin' to tell us how to live? That ain't how it works, li'l bruh. *We* get to decide how we live in here. *We* make up our own rules. And that ain't how we carry it."

They glared me down, like I was the traitor for questioning them. I suppose I was. But at the time, and I hadn't ever used this word before, I was *flabbergasted.* A law of nature had just been violated as if the sun had stopped its ascent, spun around, and scooted back into night.

I felt betrayed. They were looking at me like they'd beat my ass if I pressed the issue — and Kurt was so pleased.

In sixty seconds, I'd lost all respect for them, and in the process, I became the outcast. I felt so ashamed, though I knew I'd done nothing wrong according to the code.

"Man, y'all a bunch of fake-ass dudes," I told them. "Always talkin' about 'respect this' and 'respect that.' Talkin' about loyalty. You complain about how there ain't enough unity, but then y'all let this dude disrespect us all, and now you telling me we ain't gonna do shit about it?"

I could feel the menace emanating off them, so I said

nothing else. I stomped to my cell and basically stayed there the next few months, sulking, until I went to trial.

During that time, I kept thinking about how my whole life, I'd tried to do what the code called for — even when I was scared, even though I didn't want to most times — because I feared the consequences of not obeying: being rejected by my friends, being bullied, being labeled as weak.

But weakness appears in many guises. The more I thought about it, the more I understood it was weakness that kept me tethered to the code. All somebody had to do to get me to fight was to say that I was too scared to fight, and my fear of others thinking I was afraid (and therefore weak) would override my fear of fighting. I was a puppet.

I also saw this wasn't the first time friends of mine had bent the code to suit them. We gave our friends "passes" all the time. Kurt was their poker buddy. I'd seen them fight for lesser violations, such as somebody jumping the line in the cafeteria or spilling juice on their shoes accidentally or butting into their conversations. I'd seen them fight guys they didn't like, guys with low statuses, guys who were weak. I had, too. I felt like a sheep in wolf's clothing.

I wondered whether the Bible I'd been reading was starting to get to me.

When I came to Death Row, I saw that my new podmates generally shared the attitude of the veterans on Safekeeping. Part of it, I think, was because we know our clock is counting down, and enforcing the code means you'd go to the hole all the time — and nobody wants to spend their last days on earth in solitary. There were hard men, but they emphasized the respect element far more than the punishment part. It seemed most followed the code only when it was self-serving. The bullies used it to impose their will on the weak, to keep others from intervening, and to deter anyone from telling the cops of their crimes.

As the code's glow faded, I saw it for the dark thing it was.

Eight or nine months into my time on Death Row, I sensed the code's pressure easing off my psyche, squeezing me less and less, though I saw its fist-shaped bruises on men around me. For one thing, I was becoming adept at avoiding scenarios that exposed me to disrespect — a man would have to seek me out to start trouble. I tried to be at peace with everyone, meaning I emphasized respect from my end, and I quit preaching the code. I actually felt relieved by the hypocrisy, as if the door to my stuffy cell had opened. Instead of being so paranoid, instead of acting like a downed power line in human form, all amped up on adrenaline, I could breathe.

In the Bible, I saw another way to live. In some ways, I thought I could be both a convict and a Christian. Loving my neighbor included not disrespecting or betraying them, nor being a busybody. But when it came to punishing offenses, the two codes veered in opposite directions. I could not serve two masters; I'd have to choose one. I'd already tried the street code and convict code, and I knew their inevitable ends. I decided to let the dead bury their own.

* * *

I spent more than a year in two-down. Finally, eleven-up came open when a buddy of mine moved to another pod. Upon entering my new home, the first thing I noticed was its eye-aching brightness. Its rear-wall window faced west, so the afternoon sun lit the cell's interior.

From that window, I could see a huge swath of lush grass that ran into the perimeter wall about twenty yards away. Geese cavorted, dined, and napped on that grass; foxes, cats, and groundhogs slunk across it.

Being on the second floor, nearly level with the perimeter wall's top, I could see beyond it to trees, buildings in the city, a church steeple.

I could see a slice of sky.

But when I shut my door to use the toilet, I discovered something behind it. Crusty, whitish stains snail-trailed down the door from about waist level. *What the hell?* I thought. As I stepped to the door and glanced out its window, my eyes landed on the guard booth, directly in my line of sight. From this elevated position, I could see down into the booth, could see a guard sitting in a chair. I knew some guys loved to expose themselves to guards — or to masturbate while staring at their silhouettes in the booth.

That's when it registered: Semen stained the door's interior like a secret besetting sin.

I leapt back in revulsion, but where could I run? I'd have to deal with it. It was a lesson in Paradise Hunting: There's always a serpent lurking in a tree.

Wearing three layers of rubber gloves, *aaaaahhhhh*-ing in disgust through gritted teeth, I tied a t-shirt around my face and scrubbed at the depravity with wire pads for an hour, pinking up the dark-red door.

Afterward, I'd still see ghost stains in the paint, a slight discoloration, as if the guy's sin had burned onto the very soul of my door. I decided to move, but I'd see those stains until I left that cell.

Something else revealed itself later that afternoon. I was lying on my bunk, listening to radio stations I could now tune in to, when a glint of movement caught my attention. On the wall beside my door, light shimmered. The sun had slanted in and struck my mirror, which was warped by bolts along its edges. The sunbeam folded in upon itself like miracle origami to create what appeared to be a molten-gold angel dancing in place. Its beauty awed me.

Every day, I'd watch my angel appear, seeming to materialize from within the prison wall itself. I'd stare at it for the few minutes it retained its shape, watching as the edges de-atomized and sunk back into the cell's wall, as if the mundane world could tolerate such poetry for only so long. Since the apparition was three feet from my cell door, I'd also invariably notice the phantom stain.

That afternoon dance: a reminder of the ebb and flow of sin and salvation.

features from The List: attachments, banished, disparity, Groundhog Day, staff

21

Pretending to be Human

by George T. Wilkerson

a crowd of people,
clenched together like a fist,
walk by jabbing and hooking
fingers at the glass, whispering
behind hands with nods and shrugs
as they openly stare at the spectacle:

showering, playing chess, watching television —
men on death row continuing
tame lives, immune to these intrusions.

the crowd slips forward
toward the next exhibit, shaking its head as if

       disappointed.
a red-headed coed, seeming sheepish, glances back
and my friend presses against the Plexiglas
a homeless man's cardboard placard
on which he'd scrawled his name
in two-inch letters, and below it: WRIT ME.
"you misspelled WRITE, you idiot," i say,
good wingman that i am. he flips his sign
around to read it. blushing
prettily, grinning at our embarrassment,
the girl waves goodbye.

features from The List: banished, displayed

A Body is a Home
by George T. Wilkerson

I. Hobo Fires

some guys are sentimental hoarders, their cells plump
with life, stacked with excess everything. Düke, a six-two
    biker dude
graffitied with tattoos, papered a wall with photos, had some
    dangling
from the ceiling on a string like a mobile above a baby's crib.

he would stand amid it, imagining himself surrounded by
    mom,
Brayden, Justin, Lisa, cousins, friends, exes, even old enemies
he'd secretly forgiven. a squat, former Special Forces soldier
named Eric turned his cell into a bunker packed with a year's
    worth

of gas station snacks. some spoiled before he could eat it
    without puking —
but he ate it anyway. others keep nothing personal. except a
    cup,
toothbrush, soap, and prison-issued clothing, their cells seem
    empty.
they give the guards nothing

to hurt them with: possessions create substance, things to
    grip
and strip. they're all but invisible as individuals, blurring
    'round the edges
of our vision like wraiths that'll dissipate if gazed upon.
    erasing
themselves makes them impervious to persecution from
    officers.

we cup our souls around our stuff
like hobo fires in coffee cans. we absorb
their comfort, depend on them
for gravity and light.

II. Screws and Turnkeys

many men walk around tightly wound and twitching,
    springloaded
with vigilance when interacting with officers: "man,
I won't risk even *speaking* with him — he's too vindictive!
I don't want to be falsely accused of 'indecent exposure,'

a sex charge. or for them to toss my cell . . . I've got extra
    books."
or photos or art supplies or food. i'm anxious every time
i'm summoned to The Sarge's Office for a medical
    appointment
or to sign for mail. my heart races, my palms sweat. i
    question

whether i've pissed off a guard. i wonder if i'll return. some
don't. before guards enter our pod to search cells or arrest a
    man
they stop at the guard booth in the hall, start pulling on blue
or black latex gloves, like proctologists. we snatch furtive
    glances

through the wall of Plexiglas. we holler *MAN DOWN*
and ask ourselves *who are they coming for? did they look up
at my cell?* toilets start whooshing, swallowing whatever.
we prop in our doorways or continue walking laps as our
    eyes

track the guards: watching but not watching TV; playing but
    not
playing cards. stiff but nonchalant, scared to draw their
    attention

24

onto ourselves, in case the guards are still deciding who to
      fuck
with. i sag with relief when they screw anyone besides me.

III. Bindlesticks

i often wonder, *where will I sleep tonight?*
my current cell? broken-boned
and bloodied on a hospital bed? naked and shivering in a
      corner
of the psych ward? wearing full restraints in a holding cage

outside the hole, skin still lit and peeling
from pepper spray? being on Death Row means shit
can crack off any second. aside from death i have no release
date to look forward to, so you'd think

where i lay my head at night is set in stone. i'm permanently
confined yet feel perpetually homeless.
some men count their life as forfeit already; all they have left
is coffee, tv, non-nude porn magazines. candy bars

and fifteen-minute phone calls. outside recreation,
Bibles, Qurans, old letters, vendettas, and lotion. favorite
      objects
and activities, these seemingly insignificant freedoms and
      luxuries
are a man's only solace and consistency. each man's unique

bindlestick of attachments
displays his values
like a sticky fingerprint
of possessions, sentiments, routines.

IV. Tent City

how do i avoid the unavoidable bullshit? i don't

but the Boy Scouts prepared me for this. as a Scout, to grasp
        the basics
of wilderness survival, i first had to grapple with transience,
        the pain
and fear that's interwoven with impermanence. while hiking
        through

buzzing mosquito-infested forests, life as i knew it got left
behind. everything i carried served a practical function. after
        being
rolled up, tucked, folded, stacked, and packed, it altogether
        occupied
six cubic feet (or so my canvas rucksack advertised). an
        object's value

was the sum of its utility minus its volume and weight,
        measured
in cubic inches and ounces. the less i had, the freer i felt.
my sense of liberty kindled when i was restricted to basic
        necessities.
my ingenuity sparked to life against the simple demands of
        SURVIVAL.

one of my handiest items was twine — a fat spool of the
        sturdy kind —
for starting fires, building snares, catching fish, dangling
        food
from a tree branch, wrapping tourniquets, and general
        binding.
many things serve a higher purpose when bound. now i

camp in my cell with the square-footage of a tent. according
        to prison
policy, i should be able to fold, tuck, roll, stack, and pack
all my belongings into three boxy, flimsy white plastic
        shipping bags
(the size of brown paper grocery bags) for up to six cubic
        feet.

books: no more than ten. it takes ten books to adequately
    study
my faith, or anything really, like law books i'd need in order
    to work on
my legal appeals to get my body off Death Row. that's two-
    point-five cubic
feet of mental and Spiritual acuity for me. i own one cubic
    foot

of hygiene items, luxuries to prevent odors and rashes and to
    preserve
dignity, to soothe my itchy need to feel neat and clean. two
    more cubic
feet are crammed with my creativity: paper, pens, poetry,
    drawings,
a notebook of ideas. that leaves half a cubic foot for food and
    sentimentality.

i own a large brown envelope bulging with tattered pages
    scrawled on
by my dad before he died, and crappy-but-cute Kindergarten
    drawings
of now-teenaged nieces who swore i was the world's best
    uncle
though i was already here when they were born. i also have

a two-inch stack of photos of my brothers and me when we
    were little
boys, of our smiling parents (before divorce), of people i've
    never met
and places i've never been but are important to friends and
    relatives
and therefore important to me. that's how i fill and maintain

my six cubic feet of space, carved from a hard fucking place.
technically, then, all my food is contraband and can be
    confiscated.

to keep anything new is to also discard something old. in this
way,
i keep my life here packed up in bags that tear easily

which is fine by me because, in the end, my real treasures —
my faith, my memories, my love and creativity —
inhabit the infinite space inside my soul:
incorruptible, ethereal, eternal,

for a body is a home.

features from The List: attachments, family, mortality, staff

The Death House is No House
by Robert Johnson

The Death House is no house, really, and no home, ever, more like a funeral parlor with a long line of viewing rooms arranged in artificial habitats we call cells and they call coffins: repositories for the living dead, bodies distended, embalmed alive — pallid, sallow, doughy, defeated.

Almost no one resists when the time comes. And the time comes, it seems, with a relentlessness that is awful, leaving the condemned in a state of awe — struck dumb, made numb.

You can pretty much have the world on your side and it won't matter. Ask Troy Davis, whose 2011 case got worldwide attention. There was an unreasonable amount of reasonable doubt, no doubt about that. Didn't matter. We are all Troy Davis, reformers say, straining to understand, trying to wake up our neighbors to the madness.

We might one day be Troy Davis, and we are today and every day accountable for Troy Davis, but the folks who *are* Troy Davis — each and every one, day in and day out — are all on death row, 24/7, waiting to go, hoping the lottery passes them by for no good reason they can think of other than blind luck. Troy Davis understood that, even as his luck ran out.

features from The List: limbo, mortality

Fat Brown Quarters
by George T. Wilkerson

It's no surprise that most here find religion: When you think you're going to die, you make up your mind about what's on *the other side*. I know of no atheists here. Since we have no classes, religious services are also a type of recreation. Even in the free world, separating the true worshippers from the fake can be difficult, but on Death Row it's nearly impossible.

No doubt, many are true to what they believe, and for them their faith defines their identity, but in here, religion is contaminated by what we can *get* from it. Literally. We have so little variety and freedom, the little we do have strengthens in significance. Prison-issued anything is homogenous, monotonous, bland, devoid of personality. Even personalities can homogenize on Death Row unless one actively strives to individuate — by getting covered in bad tattoos, for instance. Religious affiliation offers a chance to stylize and spice up time since each religion gives access to exclusive privileges.

If one registers as Jewish, he can receive a "special diet" tray at meals — pre-packaged Kosher food that's relatively fresh and edible, compared to the typical prison-made grub, which often is congealed, stale, wilted.

To prevent a choke hazard — think: garrote — necklaces are prohibited. However, if registered as Catholic, one may place an order with a vendor for a fancy rosary (*could*, rather: policy has since changed). Nothing displays one's piety and class superiority like gold-fixtured, dried-blood–looking rosary beads made from compressed rose petals.

Further, Muslims get access to Kufis (knitted skullcaps) of various colors, and giving alms to less-fortunate Muslims is obligatory. So for some, the deciding factor is the stylish caps or, for the indigent, guarantee of commissary items from their brethren. Plus, they get a couple annual feasts and can brag about (or sell) the lamb chops, fried chicken, hot sauce, and delicate flaky baklava they get to eat that the rest of us don't.

Back in 2009, tobacco products were banned in state facilities, including prisons. But not for Native American practitioners, for whom tobacco is an essential element in praying. Overnight, the Native population exploded from two people to thirty. Death Row's population is about 140. Outside, lined up, as each man steps to enter the sacred prayer circle, the chaplain hands him a medicine cup containing a teaspoon of tobacco pressed into its bottom like a fat brown quarter. They can smoke it in their pipes, burn it in their smudge pots, sprinkle shreds of it into the wind — or secretly smuggle it back inside and sell it for a dollar per roll-up. They can easily get five bucks for that teaspoon: that's twenty ramen soups, twenty-five coffees, or eight stamps; for the druggies, that's five pills; for the perverted, a blowjob. They also have an annual feast they can brag about or sell items from.

We can register with only one faith group at a time but are permitted to change faiths every three to four months. That alone should tell you something about the waxing and waning of devotion on Death Row, about our concerns with living life *now* versus fearing what will happen *after* life. Often when one changes religions, his former faith's paraphernalia — now considered contraband by prison policy — finds its way to the black market. Native American headbands and Tupperware sacred-items boxes; prayer rugs and Kufis and Rasta caps; thick Bible dictionaries, prayer beads, and shiny crucifixes. It's all for sale. I've had guys, seven or eight transactions removed, try to sell me the same Bible concordance I sold ten years ago.

Back when they banned tobacco, I registered as Native American so I could smoke and sell tobacco three days a week. I did this for years, despite being a professed Christian. Eventually, I felt so guilty for acting like an idolater that I left The Circle and registered as a Protestant. That first Sunday rolled around, and I had no intention of attending church services with some I knew to be hypocrites. Lying in bed, fiending for a cigarette, I heard a voice in my head that I attribute to God. He sounds sorta like Charleston Heston in that old-ass movie in which he played Moses: deep, authoritative voice, slightly ironic tone. He said, "You went outside to smoke three times a week for an hour at a time for three years straight, and missed not one day. In the rain. In the freeze. In the scorch. In the ants. You skipped weekly movies. You skipped recreation. You went through strip searches . . . And you can't go to church twice a week because of the hypocrites? So there weren't any hypocrites in The Circle? Well, maybe not, not now, not since *you* quit going."

I got out of bed and went to church. I haven't missed a day since, even after we Christians lost our annual feasts we used to humble-brag about. And I no longer pass judgment on who's authentic and who's a hypocrite because I realize that despite being a sincere worshipper, I often do things to make this hard life a little softer — which from an outside perspective probably makes me look fake as hell. Even so, I'm a Christian, meaning I'm *forgiven*, not flawless.

And to demonstrate my devotion, I own the most expensive Bible in our small congregation: ornate, leatherbound, and handmade (in China).

features from The List: attachments, calendars, idle, mortality

Witness
by Robert Johnson

My son was born in the morning, days before the execution.
I was there at his birth, amid
the blood and gore and
tears of joy.

>He cried, I cried, and
>the world opened before him.

The condemned man was killed as midnight approached.
I was there in the Death House, amid the
blanched flesh and the yawning, gasping mouth,
the vacant lifeless eyes.

>He died, no one cried, and
>the world closed around him.

I couldn't help but think of them
together —
dearly arrived, dreadfully departed —
bookends, brackets
around the day,
around existence,

>each marked by a certificate
>routine, unremarkable, "certified"

I couldn't help but think of the man before me
swaddled in denim, strapped to the gurney
an overgrown baby, really, abandoned

>by family
>by the world

nameless at the end
a prison number

delivered unto death
in our name.

features from The List: banished, family, staff

Part II: Everyday

The Huggy Boys:
Letter to My Mom, 2011
by George T. Wilkerson

Dear Mom,

You are so funny! At least, I assume you were joking when you asked whether I ever get to hug anyone. If you were serious, then I think you forget where I am. There are nothing but men here, and we're too tough for hugs!

But, now that you ask, I do miss *your* hugs (and your kimchi). I miss wrapping you up and making you groan as I squeezed — how your back would pop-pop-pop.

We may not hug on death row, but we do shake hands *a lot.* We're pretty much confined to our pods all day, except for when we go to the mess hall for meals, to outside recreation, or to a religious service, so we don't get much opportunity to socialize with others. However, in greeting and in parting is when all the handshaking happens.

For example, in church service on Sundays, it's become a sort of Spiritual ritual. As about twenty of us stream in from various pods, every single one of us shakes hands with everyone else, weaving in and out of the crowd. From above, I'd bet it looks like an elaborate dance, accompanied by murmurs of "God bless you" or "Peace and blessings" or "Peace, Brother." It is the same coming and going. To call it excessive is an understatement: If twenty of us show up, that means I'll shake hands nineteen times, twice — so thirty-eight times! It's a little embarrassing to think about it now.

Let's say a pod of men is lined up in the hall for commissary. If I happen to be returning from a sick-call appointment and pass by that line, one of two things will occur. I will either greet some of the guys individually or acknowledge them all at once with a nod or wave and keep it moving. If I choose to acknowledge specific people, everyone sees the closeness of each friendship. Well, mostly, as not everybody here assigns meaning to different types of greetings — but many of us do, or are at least aware of the implicit meanings. I might just nod to one guy, fist-bump another, shake hands with the next, pull the hand-clasp-into-a-half-hug with another. Each signifies a degree of familiarity and closeness. To not even nod or acknowledge one with a word is to say *you are invisible to me*, which is an insult I've seen guys take offense to. One of the worst things you can do to a man in here is to deem them nonexistent. We get that enough from the world outside.

Back when I first got here, having been around gangs, having been in cliques, I figured all the handshaking was a typical feature of social hierarchy. You know how it is. I still think that's part of it, but it doesn't explain how widespread it is, nor how excessively we do it. Before and after *every* meal? *Every* service? *Every* rec period? Perhaps it speaks to something deeper, more universal to human needs. Maybe we aren't as hard and indifferent to being alone as we pretend to be.

Anyway, I love you, Mom. Please tell Sara to write me next time she calls or comes to visit you from college.

Your son,
George

features from The List: banished, idle, masks, segregation, static

Circadian Rhythm
by Robert Johnson

He awakens, drinks
in the familiar stench
notes the order of things in his cell
     steel toilet encroaching
     solid door encasing
     cement walls embracing
an empty shelf that feels like an indictment
of his empty life.

He breathes deep
the raw wounds of loss, lament
then retreats back into
the soul-saving stupor of sleep.

Wake me when it's over
he thinks

     knowing the day will come too soon.

features from The List: Groundhog Day, limbo, mortality

Clorox

by George T. Wilkerson

5:42 AM, still dark in his cell
on the anniversary of his crime. he'd begin
his ritual of remembering.
shut his eyes, lay back on his bunk, see again

one young man's mother fight to breathe
through sobs and snot
when she testified at his trial. he told me
his own mom had wept the same way as his death

sentence was delivered. *my mom too*, i said. technically he'd
     live
'til cancer took his husk twenty years later. 6 AM, the lights
would buzz and flicker. he'd sigh, rise, rinse his eyes
then look in his mirror. he'd alternate their names

with apologies: Brian – *i'm sorry* – Dylan – *i'm sorry* –
Brian – *i'm sorry* – Dylan – *i'm sorry*. he voiced their names
aloud but kept his apologies silent, knowing nobody
wanted to hear them. still, the verbal rosary

he prayed through ((Brian – *i'm sorry* –
Dylan – *i'm sorry*)) as he studied his tired eyes
and the new lines that come with growing
old on Death Row. i promised him to always remember

this vivid dream he described to me several times
in which he was that mother
praying through her anguish
in her son's bedroom. i may not recall

the exact words of her prayers, but i swear
i will never forget the scene and what it felt like

to open myself to her emptiness:
i can still smell his sweat.

this room will always be his
hovel though no longer so
disheveled. well, except for these
two dents on his blanket

that my elbows like to lay in
when i pray. Lord, look here,
Lord, right here
at this blank spot

between where my elbows go — right here
where my tears done bleached
the color off these covers. Lord,
it's been sixteen years —

how much longer is it gonna hurt?
how much longer, Lord?
how much longer? Lord, have mercy
on me. have mercy

on her, Lord,
have mercy
on us. here
he always found himself

on his knees
muttering through his rosary
of names and apologies
before he started his day.

features from The List: calendars, family, grief

43

Pod People
by Robert Johnson

Human husks wrapped in scorn
solitary figures, mute, forlorn
each utterly alone
in a terminal cell
in the cold shadow of the Death House.

The to-be-dead, the living dead
(if you can call this living)
lay flat, unmoving, unmourned
arms crossed, faces slack
eyes half open, glazed, black
tortured on a modern rack
we call death row.

Buzzers beep, hum, a morning rite
inert figures come to life,
in a manner of speaking,
a marionette review
        run in mime
        lost in time.

Over go pairs of feet
thwack, thwack
flat on the floor
Slowly rises each torso
twisting, creaking
turning gingerly toward the door

        in search of release,
        settling for surcease, for
        pain dissolved in medication, given
        daily to numb the soul
        maintain control in this

dark version of Groundhog Day.

Yet each man, each day, in his way
goes the distance, makes his bones
traverses his cloistered world alone
pacing his cell, his private hell
dancing with his demons
dreaming of lost freedoms
finding hope where he can
          when he can,
          if he can

each yearning for Redemption
to be Somebody who counts
not just Some Body
to be counted.

features from The List: banished, grief, Groundhog Day,
mental health

Lights Out
by Robert Johnson

Years of living alone leeched
the complexion from her skin, left her face
pale as her cell's concrete floor
She can barely be called a person
of color anymore. Stooped now, she paces
daily, nightly, ever so lightly
hiding in plain sight
barely visible now
in the afterglow
of lights out
on death row.

Note: As of 2022, all but a few states have a Death Row that is segregated: The prisoners are essentially in the hole for ten, twenty, thirty years until they win their appeals, die, or get executed. North Carolina's Death Row is a congregated setting, where prisoners may interact with each other during the day.

features from The List: banished, grief, limbo, segregation

The Knowledge of Good and Evil
by George T. Wilkerson

scene: Death Row; a Christmas
tree, ornamented, tinseled, well-lit,
complete with phony gifts beneath.
it crowds one

half of the hall as we shoulder on
around, en route to and from chow.
most guys walk on by — eyes ahead —
but some press

in close to thump a tiny colored lightbulb
hard enough to darken it,
                              pinch needles into zees
or brazenly slap the crap out of plastic dec-

orations, as if to say *i'm hurting
you because you're hurting me.*
still other men *ooooo* and *aaahh*
like little kids eyeing mint-condition

memories that are kept shelved
except for special occasions. despite
my grief, the Lord is my strength —

                              i shall not want

or fear the sparkling ghosts
of Christmases past.
Christmas morning, a burly guard
stands there peering deep

into our tree's depth of plastic branches
then grabs it roughly, angrily even,
and shake-shake-shakes the fuck out of it

((like I imagine he does to his wife

and kids)), rattling off a noisy mess
of decorations. the guard scans the wreckage,
assuming our anxious reactions
mean we hid something dangerous, monsters

that we are. seeing nothing,
he looks right at us,
shrugs, and says, "Okay,
you guys are straight

for now. Go to chow." then, he goosesteps
over scattered ornaments, turning a sharp corner
into the office as we hurry to rebuild
the dignity of our tree.

features from The List: banished, calendars, grief, staff

Keep It Moving
by George T. Wilkerson

In 2016, while sitting on my bunk, I heard several guys hollering "MAN DOWN!" — our signal that an officer was entering our pod. My ears perked up: a door slamming shut, then another, unintelligible conversation, an outburst of cursing, and someone yelling, "I don't see why y'all gotta punish *all* of us for what only *one* man did!"

That got me up and to my door.

My cell is in the corner of the L-shaped tier. Stepping out, I could see the entire fifty-foot by seventy-foot dayroom, where a black-suited officer stood out amid all the red. She leaned against our red stairway's red railing, explaining to four or five guys wearing faded red jumpsuits why she shut and locked our two janitor's closets. Then, she exited through our pod's sally-port door and pivoted left into the next pod.

The men who'd heard the news directly from the officer made their way around to share it with the rest of us, already embellishing the incident. A fifty-ish, beefy white guy wearing a too-small gray t-shirt and faded black nylon shorts (our approved informal attire) — and who relished bearing bad news — lumbered toward me on the tier. His face wore a fake-grave expression. He hadn't been near the officer but had heard from his neighbor, and he immediately came to tell me for some reason.

He was shaking his head. "Well, looks like we ain't gonna be able to use our closets' faucets for hot water no more — you know some guys'll die without their hot water."

Ah: I got my hot water for coffee from the closet; he was fishing for a response, still shaking his head but grinning.

I draped my forearms over the railing and cocked my head at the TV, which was high on the Plexiglas front wall across the pod. Refusing to look at him, I tried to embody indifference, even as his presence irritated me.

"Yeah," he continued, "we gonna have to use our own sinks, and they don't get as hot . . . "

"What happened, man?" I cut him off. I already knew the implications of not having access to our closets.

His grin widened, and his enthusiasm shone. "I mean, don't get me wrong. I get why somebody'd want to hit the ejection switch, but why make it harder on all of us? That's some selfish shit. Right? Anyway, today she said that Juda — that short guy with the scraggly beard?"

"What? He *died?*"

"Well, now wait, she ain't said that *exactly.* I heard she said he hung his neck in the janitor closet up on his pod."

"Did he die or not?"

"I don't know. I doubt it. But probably. Now we gotta find somewhere else to get our—"

I didn't let him finish. I went into my cell, stretched the dingy bedsheet I used as a privacy screen across my doorway, and plopped on my bunk in a small rage not just because of this asshole but also the administration. Typical. The no-more-closet rule was a knee-jerk reaction. How could it stop a man bent on suicide? He would just find another route.

The next morning on the way to breakfast, I saw a half-dozen men crowded by the sergeant's office asking whether Juda was going to be okay. The duty sergeant told them to calm down, that Juda had survived and had been sent to Mental Health. Someone sucked their teeth, and they all went on to chow, shaking their heads. We all knew what happened on Mental Health, from first-hand experience.

My stress level was peaking, and I wasn't alone. Our cleaning supplies were in those closets; we all had certain times we used them. On my pod, we'd had an informal cleaning schedule that spread across the day between 7 a.m. and 11 p.m., which is how long we're allowed out of our cells. Now, we had from 7 a.m. to 9 a.m., and for thirty minutes during that span, we'd be at breakfast. It takes about ten minutes to do just a half-decent job cleaning one's cell. Guys who usually slept in the mornings now had to get up and join the rest of us rushing to the closets, jostling for position, trying to establish a hierarchy of access.

Tension charged the air, crackling like static as we walked around rubbing each other the wrong way. The locked closets disrupted whole days, broke circadian rhythms, restructured routines and relationships. When you have little in the way of freedoms, the few you have multiply in significance.

Over the next few weeks of readjustment, petty arguments erupted over nothing and everything. At recreation, we were more aggressive during our already notoriously rough basketball and volleyball games. There was a spike in sports-related injuries: twisted knees, cracked ankles, herniated discs, torn rotator cuffs. I had bruises up and down my body from colliding through the net with opponents. We exercised to exhaustion. I woke up in the middle of the night to crank out push-ups, sit-ups, squats. Angry faces paced the yard and pod or did wind-sprints outside.

For me, it was to distract myself; the suicide attempt had reintroduced me to despair. I didn't want to see it, or think about it, and most definitely didn't want to *feel* it. I withdrew back into myself. My conversations drifted off; I quit socializing so much. I noticed others doing the same. We locked in our cells early, to be alone. It was a reminder not to make friends. But I knew I'd have to face my demon.

One night, I lay on my bunk and closed my eyes to think. Someone's words echoed in my head: *I get why someone'd hit the ejection switch, but why make it harder on all of us?*

Part of me agreed that because we're so intertwined here, we owe certain considerations to each other, so I resented Juda because he had known how his action would create complications. Nearly ten years prior, someone else had succeeded where he had failed — and it had taken us years to convince staff to return all-day closet access to us. Then again, he'd been in a dark place if the thought of dying sooner was preferable to being executed later, as the decades in-between are worse than death itself. It's difficult to consider others' inconveniences in that state. And besides, where does our prevalent attitude of indifference factor into this?

I still hadn't quite come to terms with my own death sentence, with the likelihood I'd spend the last of my life in prison anticipating my own demise, with the fact that one day I'd forcibly be strapped to a gurney while wearing a diaper as a salt-based poison flooded my bloodstream like liquid napalm to burn me to death in front of a dozen witnesses who'd watch me writhing — some gladly, some sadly, as the audience would include family members from both sides of the crime. Suicidal thoughts were stapled to my death sentence. Even before my trial, though, I had attempted suicide, slitting my own throat and wrists. After coming to Death Row, the suicidal thoughts persisted, although my reasons for wanting to die would vary.

I had wanted and needed to speak with someone, but how could I? Suicide's considered a feature of weakness and instability, which, admittedly, perfectly described my mental state. I couldn't bear the stigma I believed would brand me as easy prey. The contempt. The averted eyes and ridicule.

I also couldn't afford to jeopardize my escape route by confiding in someone, only to have him gossip, eventually landing my story in the lap of staff — and me on Mental Health: naked, shivering, humiliated, in an empty cell with nothing but my torment. Last time, I'd had to see a team of shrinks each day to earn back a scrap of clothing and piece of decency. Underwear on Day 3. Day 4 was socks. T-shirt, Day 5. It took more than a week to get dressed, much longer to recover my sense of dignity. A camera that live-fed to the nurses' station perched like Poe's grim black raven above the door to monitor when I pissed, shit, cried, paced, masturbated, paced, wept, raved. Its red eye didn't blink, it winked: This "evaluation process" was ostensibly designed to facilitate recovery; rather, it served to deter future half-assed attempts. I'd decided that if there *were* a next time, I would succeed — instead of re-experiencing that haunted hall lined with cells on either side, reverberating with the din of lunatics, the air thick with the scent of unwashed bodies, sweat, bodily fluids, excrement, fear. So no, I couldn't discuss it. Already, the risk of failure was high; there's no easy way to die on Death Row.

At least once a day for a decade, I scanned my catalog of death methods. I'd absorbed strength from my preparations like a man with a powerful secret, hiding lightning in my pocket. No matter how desperate I got, no matter how much this prison stripped from me, I could at least decide my time and method of death.

My eyes popped open. Lying there on my bunk, I couldn't remember the last time I'd considered suicide. I figured it'd been a year or more. After thousands and thousands of days, consecutive days, I had stopped. Why?

I sat up and looked around my cell, as if my answer was there, somewhere.

*   *   *

Death Row is unique within the prison system in North Carolina. We aren't shipping in or out regularly. For the most part, our population is static, with the rare newcomer or departure. We live shoulder-to-shoulder for ten, fifteen, twenty, thirty years, and gradually this *me versus them* mentality I'd walked in with melted away, leaving only *us.*

We eat together, pray together, elbow each other's teeth out on the basketball court, borrow and lend books and magazines, teach each other to draw, play chess, write poetry. When one of us dies, it's like losing a digit, a limb. A friend.

In other words, I realized I'd started to care. I could see Divine Providence at work, orchestrating a slow transformation in me: the close-quartered living arrangements, my friendships teaching me how to actively empathize, using my essays and poetry to confront my flaws, and especially our creative writing class because we read aloud what we wrote, sharing our stories like communion. It showed me how similar our pre-prison lives were — the poverty, the dysfunctional families, the addictions. It showed me that our differences were circumstantial or superficial, but beneath it all — or, rather, above it all — we were all the same: human. The more I saw we shared in common, the more I cared for the common good. Unconsciously, I had come to view death row as a community that I was a member of.

I was no longer suicidal.

It seems all those handshakes were paying off.

Whatever the cause, I wanted Juda to feel connected too, hoping it would help him like it'd helped me. Yet I couldn't deny still feeling irritated that he had complicated our lives, even thinking that he deserved what he got — which suggested I hadn't changed much after all since it was a self-centered and insensitive perspective. It was clear that at best, I'd only ever be a work in progress. I didn't fully want to help Juda, but intellectually, I thought I ought to; thus, I couldn't tell if my "compassion" was just my way of wrapping myself in a comforting lie or whether I was genuinely concerned for his psychological well-being. Although the end result was the same, the motive mattered to me. What did it mean that I had mixed motives, both selfish and unselfish reasons for wanting to somehow help?

This still left a question: What could I possibly do, anyway?

*   *   *

In the meantime, after months of nervous excitement, the phones became operational. Until 2016, we'd been allowed only one ten-minute phone call at Christmas. Now, there was a phone on our pod that we could use whenever we wanted — for a fee, but still, it suddenly felt a lot less crowded in here.

It'd been years since I'd last used the phone. I felt like a virgin on my wedding night: eager to put this thing to use, not sure if it'd hurt, scared I'd screw something up. It was the most alive I'd felt since coming to Death Row.

Shortly after he returned from Mental Health, I spotted Juda through the Plexiglas windows separating our dining halls. He was slouched against the rear wall while everyone else sat eating together at the four-way stainless steel tables. He looked deflated; his eyes were on the floor. His posture spoke of shame, isolation, defeat. I knew that posture well.

But I didn't know his reasons for attempting suicide, and maybe it had nothing at all to do with feeling alienated. Maybe nothing I could say or do would make the least difference. Still, I felt compelled to try, to do something in addition to praying.

Since he was on a third floor pod and I was on the first, having a conversation with him was going to be unlikely. So I sent him a note through one of his podmates who attended church with me. In part, I said, "I see you. You have my sympathy. But I don't know what else to do . . . Just know that I don't judge you. Rather, I see myself when I look at you. I don't consider you weak or unstable, only human." And I shared some of my story about my own suicidal tendency.

Sometimes, when one of our pods is in the commissary line, either Juda or I will walk by — returning from recreation or a sick call — and we'll make eye contact. We never say anything, but just that look says it all: *You are not alone.* And it's enough.

We both nod, straighten our spines, and keep it moving.

features from The List: banished, diminished, grief, masks, mental health, mortality, staff, static

Last Night Lullaby
by Robert Johnson

Goodnight moon
Goodnight gloom
Goodnight to my lonely tomb

Goodnight cell
Goodnight smell
Goodnight screams of man and bell
Goodnight to my crimson hell

Goodnight tears that each night fall
Quietly, privately, on our pillows
Hidden from the other fellows
Weeping, too, for dreams gone fallow

Goodnight moon
Goodnight gloom
Goodnight to my steel cocoon
Tomorrow brings release from loss, sin
A new life, I pray, will bloom again

features from The List: grief, mortality

Part III: Everyone

Talking to My Mom in Autumn, 2016
by George T. Wilkerson

so many damned layers in-between
us. "YOU HAVE A PREPAID CALL FROM
[George Wilkerson]
AN INMATE AT CENTRAL PRISON . . ."
a digital guard tells my mother, who
must PRESS 5 to accept it. how
can she ever accept my being
on death row?   "hello?" i probe
the ether. "Hi!" says she's delighted
at the same time her monotone is just
room temperature. her cute Korean-tinted
English catalogs fresh mundanities: how it now
takes all day to rake away crunchy leaves, especially
since my siblings are too busy to visit, or help;
how fast her heart flutters when she texts
a man my age she's never even met; how
she laments her creaky knees and dying
vegetable garden. her voice lies
wrinkled palms on my chest
and the inside of me
aches then opens,
presses 5,
swallows up. heat
blooms on my bones
soft as cotton pajamas.

features from The List: diminished, family, grief

Flesh is Weak

by Robert Johnson

The old men flaunt faded tattoos that once
sang loudly of boisterous youths long gone,
now pale remnants of better days, marooned
on bony arms and heaving, rolling, swollen guts.

Daggers once held firm, seemingly at the ready,
now rendered comical, creased and creviced in aging flesh.
Guns, too, both bulging biceps and the bulleted kind,
holstered and hidden deep beneath layers of fatty flesh.
Names of mothers, girlfriends, wives, children, old
neighborhoods, all once celebrated, now stretched,
warped, ravaged by age.

The spirit is willing
but the flesh is weak
no match for serving time
without end . . .
without calendar
or court date
or hope of release.

A clock with no hands
an endless circle.

These are men in decline
marked by prison life,
for life, even if they escape
their death sentences.

features from The List: calendars, limbo, mortality

The Infiltrator

by George T. Wilkerson

our new Writing Therapy
instructor was a limp beanpole-of-a-man
— easily snappable by a stiff wind —
had sleepy eyes and a ferret's way

of lounging bonelessly in his chair.
about twenty of us men
on death row sat in a circle
with him, our eyes wide and stiff.

he said, "I'm here to help you
guys tell your stories—" one of us smacked our teeth
and cut him off immediately
with a dismissive handflip

and, "man, ain't nobody
tryin' to hear what we got to say.
and it ain't gonna change nothing anyway."
beanpole snapped straight, tilted forward,

eyes ablaze. we recoiled in the face
of his sudden heat. "No, let me
tell *you* something. I stand outside
with those protestors every time

there's an execution. Every. Time.
A cop came up to us once
and asked why we do it
when it ain't gonna change

or stop executions. I told him
I don't do it thinking it'll change
what's about to happen — no,

63

I stand out there shivering in the night

because if I don't
it'll change something *in me.*
I don't want this thing
that makes me human

to die." he beat his chest
twice, then sat back.
neither did we
want to die before our bodies

and so we wrote.
and so i write.

Note: Later, after our teacher got arrested for protesting, the prison revoked his permission to come back inside.

features from The List: banished, staff

Snakes and Thunder
by George T. Wilkerson

"Well, this oughta be interesting," I said to Big Lee, my tablemate at lunch. "They posted a talent show sign-up sheet in the hall."

"Yeah?" he smirked. "Well, I ain't signing up — but I know who will."

I knew, too. It was 2017, and given that our population on North Carolina's death row consisted of about 140 men, and that most of us had been there for fifteen to twenty-five years, we knew who was who.

And Jimmy Jam of the Morgan Fam was a shameless attention-monger who would almost certainly be signing up for the talent show.

"Why're we even doing one, anyway?" I asked. "It's not like we'll get access to props. No radios or keyboards or . . . "

I couldn't think of anything else — I'd never actually seen a talent show.

"I've heard people begging Dr. Kuhns for one ever since he started these classes and stuff. Plus, they always like to see a brotha tapdancin', bojanglin', and belittlin' hisself," said Big Lee. A short, power-lifting tank of a man, he saw racism as the secret motivator for everything.

Many of us here had been arrested between the ages of eighteen and twenty-five. Now, decades down the line, guys lamented their wasted potential: *I shoulda done* ____ or *If I get a chance, I'll* ____ or *I coulda been a star!*

On my way out of the mess hall, I looked at the flyer to see who had signed up so far. Sure enough, eight of the ten names were ones I'd expected.

Most of the talents were verbal — singing, rapping, spoken word. Not surprising, since we weren't allowed access to educational programs to develop any latent skills or teach new ones. But we could sing and talk all we wanted. Jerzy said he would be performing as a "Renasaince Man" (his misspelling), and Jimmy Jam wrote, "I sing and dance and rap and juggle all at once," having to bend his talents up the side of the page to fit them beside his name. I rolled my eyes.

I checked again on the way back from dinner. A few more people had signed up, but several names had been viciously scratched out. I figured they didn't want to be associated with it if Jerzy and Jimmy Jam were involved.

Over the two weeks leading up to the show, hardly anyone mentioned it. "Are you going to the talent—" I'd try to ask, before people cut me off with a silent but vehement head shake or a "Man, I ain't watching that bullshit." Many felt that men like Jimmy Jam were stuck in denial and needed to accept our harsh reality. Others saw the attention-seeking as disgraceful, degrading, an embarrassment to us all. What one of us did, good or bad, tended to reflect on all of us in the eyes of outsiders, so guys were distancing themselves.

Since death row effectively serves as a mental health unit — the majority of us are diagnosed with mental disorders — many of our activities are considered "therapy." In fact, it's been only since 2013 that we've been given *any* therapeutic activities, and prison administrators were actively working behind the scenes to shut them down. After all, we'd been told many times point-blank, "You are *not* here to be rehabilitated." We are here to be executed. We didn't know it yet, but the talent show would be one of our last activities.

But if Writing Therapy helps us express ourselves coherently, and Meditation Therapy helps us navigate prison's inherent stress, then what would a therapeutic talent show target? Validation? Our sense of self-worth?

Dr. Kuhns, head of outpatient treatment for Death Row, felt that prescribing medication should be only one aspect of mental health treatment plans, if done at all. Before he'd arrived in 2013, prescribing medication had been the only treatment — it was about sedation, not treatment. Dr. Kuhns immediately started therapeutic activities.

I asked him what his goal was for the talent show. With characteristically cryptic conviction, he said, "It's a community-building activity."

It brought to mind an old saying: "Familiarity breeds contempt." That was the downside of being cooped up with the same faces for twenty, thirty years, against one's will. I supposed we *could* use some community building, but I was openly skeptical. Here was a bad sign: The prison staff had posted an "invitation list" for the event, perhaps because they'd heard rumors of an empty audience.

Normally, at any kind of special activity, it's standing-room only. When our Drama Therapy group staged *12 Angry Men*, we had to perform five or six shows because so many Death Row prisoners, officers, nurses, and even delegations from other prisons wanted to see it. The talent show, on the other hand, was beginning to look like a total fiasco.

I groaned knowing my name was on the invitation list. That's what I got for advocating therapeutic programs. I was one of the special ones who got to watch the talent show. Yay.

As I walked into the cavernous room where the show was being held, I saw sixty or seventy chairs. Dr. Kuhns had brought a handful of his colleagues and interns, who clumped together in the front left row. There were five empty rows behind them.

Us prisoners — who, counting the "talent," rolled perhaps thirty deep — took up the front three rows on the right side.

Let the show begin!

Dr. Kuhns, a lanky, middle-aged man wearing his usual khakis and sweater-vest-over-button-down combo, walked to the front.

"Greetings, greetings!" he said. "I'd like to welcome everyone to death row's first-ever talent show! We have seven amazing performances for you.

"You'll notice," he went on, "that I distributed instruments: some plastic-egg maracas called 'noisemakers,' a few sets of mini-bongo drums, a tambourine. To welcome each performer, we will *make some noise* — and afterward, we'll thank them . . . with more noise! But please, don't make any noise *during* the performances.

"Okay! First up is Terrance!"

Dr. Kuhns' voice echoed in the half-filled space.

Nothing.

"I know I saw him earlier," Dr. Kuhns said. "Terrance? Anyone seen Terrance?"

More silence. Everyone looked around uncomfortably.

"Uh, well, okay then. Our next performer iiisss . . . Cerron! Cerron, please come on up."

A short man who I knew to be around forty years old but who looked fifteen popped out of his chair and crept to the front, holding an eleven-by-fourteen-inch canvas.

"Let's welcome Cerron!" Dr. Kuhns shouted again, with obvious relief.

Suddenly, all hell broke loose. It sounded like a tribal war party celebrating victory. The maracas became a pit of pissed off rattlesnakes, and the bongo drums shoved thunder around the room. The prison's concrete, steel, and Plexiglas created perfect echo chamber acoustics.

Dr. Kuhns scanned the audience as if trying to impose order through sheer force of will. After a minute or so, he thrust up his hands and hollered, only we couldn't hear him. Nevertheless, we knew the frantic hand gestures for "cut the shit." It took another minute for the noise to trickle to a stop.

That was fun, I thought as we quieted. Dr. Kuhns retreated to his seat.

Cerron cringed and hugged his drawing to his chest. Looking apologetic, he said, "Uh, I actually didn't sign up for this, but Ms. Jordan told me I had to be here because not enough people signed up." He pointed accusingly at a woman sitting next to Dr. Kuhns. She brought her hands up to hide her face, then quickly forced them into her lap.

"Anyway, I brought this drawing. Here," Cerron said, and handed it to someone in the front row. "Pass it around." He started toward his seat.

Ms. Jordan gesticulated wildly for him to come back. "Cerron! Tell them what it is!"

"They can tell what it is!"

"Tell them what it *means!* You've got ten minutes!"

"Ten minutes?! You only said I had to—"

"Cerron. Tell. Them. What. It. Means. Now."

Cerron paused. "Uh, well . . . it's the Black Lives Matter movement." He spat it out like one big word, then took his seat defiantly.

Without further ado, Dr. Kuhns sprang back to the front. "Let's thank Cerron — with only thirty seconds of noise — for sharing his *amazing* drawing!"

The clamoring snakes and thunder again. When our time was up, Dr. Kuhns raised his hands like a shaman calling down a miracle. "Okay, please just *clap* to welcome Jerzy, our next performer."

Maybe four people clapped.

Jerzy calls himself many things: a genius autodidact polymath, a five-hundred-pound legal gorilla, a virtuoso, a ladies' man. He's maybe sixty years old, his shoulders stooped and his skin dusty; a pair of coke bottle glasses ride his half-nose, the other half of which was bitten off in a fight years ago. He wore this devilish grin that seemed to say, "You *have* to listen to me now."

In a jazz-lounge voice, he said, "I'm an impresario, so I'll be doing impressions of historical figures, as well as quotes and soundbites of songs."

I thought an impresario was someone who organizes events and had nothing to do with impressions, but I could be wrong.

Jerzy began singing a line or two from Frank Sinatra and Fats Domino, and "imitating" Winston Churchill and Martin Luther King, Jr. by stating one of their famous quotes. All the voices were his own, though: undeviatingly raspy and off-key. At least he got the words right, as far as we could tell.

After the first snippet, he shot us a grin and stood there silent and expectant.

We all peeped at one another, snickering, until Ms. Jordan gave an appreciative "Oh!" and clapped. Jerzy nodded. After each snippet, he awaited his applause. We clapped obediently. About six minutes into it, you could almost hear the bucket scraping the bottom of the well. Jerzy stopped, as if lost, then —

"Thank you, thank you, thank you," he said, bowing around the room with what looked like genuine tears in his eyes. Was it nostalgia for the thrill of performance, or simply the human attention? After all, he *had* spent years in solitary, off and on.

The next act was by a very tall man with heavy dreadlocks that swept his waist. He sang a ballad he'd written about coming to prison and losing his girl. While he crooned, quite movingly, he floated toward three female psychiatrists sitting with Dr. Kuhns. His fist clenched an invisible microphone under his chin, while his other hand held his heart and his eyes gripped theirs. They fake-swooned. Many of us verged on tears remembering our own wives and girlfriends.

Snakes and thunder washed our pain away. Dr. Kuhns gave us a couple minutes.

A rap duo was next, but only one person had shown up, so then Jimmy Jam's name was called.

Also over sixty, Jimmy Jam was wearing a raggedy green jacket over his faded red jumpsuit, and a beat-up green hat to match, making him look like a clown without makeup.

"I'm Jimmy Jam of the Morgan Fam, and I rap and sing and dance," he said, gyrating his hips obscenely. "And *juggle!*"

From out of nowhere, he produced three partially rotten oranges that he'd likely smuggled out of the mess hall and, from their dented appearance, had been practicing with.

While clumsily juggling and swiveling, he rapped, "I once met James Brown / when he came to town / because my cousin Juanita / and him slept around."

"Sit yo ass down!" someone in the audience added to the rhyme.

"Hey you clown / don't tell me sit down / I got ten minutes / I'm gonna use 'em . . . If you don't like Jimmy Jam / you kiss Jimmy Jam's ass!"

As he rapped, he didn't miss a beat or a hip-thrust, though he did drop an orange. Unfazed, he took off his hat, put it on his shoe, kicked it up in the air, and ducked under to catch it on his head, all the while gyrating with his mouth wide open and clapping his hands.

By now, we were laughing hysterically, some with him, some *at* him. Nevertheless, after more than forty years in prison, this was finally his MOMENT.

My god, I thought. *We're gonna have to hear him brag about this for years.*

The noisemaking time had by that point grown to three or four minutes, and the snakes and thunder burst to life again.

But something happened. The bongo drums synchronized, the beat bobbing up and down in tandem, while the maracas and hand-claps wove together to support them. We had become one.

For the next half hour, we made real music; we throbbed and pulsed with it, everyone swaying in unison. We'd found a sort of sacred fire to gather around, dancing and grinning. There was no need for words.

When I glanced over at Dr. Kuhns, he was looking at me and nodding, as if to confirm that this had all been part of his plan.

If only this could last.

features from The List: grief, idle, mental health, staff, static

Any Day Now
by George T. Wilkerson

a couple of my friends used to live
in a house near railroad tracks.

periodically, emerging from dark forest
in a drunken stupor, men got cut in half

after tripping and sprawling trying to cross.
instead of chainlink or planks of privacy

fencing, their backyard was hemmed in by twenty tons
of deadly noise. yet they hardly noticed

the bloodstained rocks and grass or when
the walls shook and their beer rattled

and tapdanced across the table
toward me. though i cringed and fidgeted

they simply braced hand against bottle
and waited for the cut

across our conversation to pass.   shrugging,
they said, "you can get used to anything."

"shiiit, not me," i'd laughed uneasily. despite living
on Death Row these last fifteen years, i am still

shaken by the prison racket: industrial-grade
air systems and stainless steel toilets
                                        *WHOOSH*ing; hissing

pistons slamming heavy iron doors
open and shut; and men   trying to holler across

72

the top of it all. worse is the clattering
reminder stirred by over-medicated buddies

on my block, staggering up the stairs
and down the tier toward their cells, clutching blindly

at anything sturdier than them — a passing arm, the hem
of somebody's shirt, the leg of their cell's plastic chair

as they crawl toward their bunk — just wishing
to sprawl safely. sometimes, as if dead

on their feet, their bodies buckle, unresponsive
as we drag them to their cells. quieter

are the fidgeting hands
and minds of those who brace

with poker cards or television,
Bibles, Qurans, even apathy

against the rumbling of our own death
sentences, sealed in

by concrete, steel, and Plexiglas.

*features from The List: attachments, diminished, mental
health, mortality*

Black Prison Nation
by Robert Johnson

At first blush, today's Black prisons
look like green wounds, a fresh assault, where
money means justice
        and race costs dearly.

But *Old Hannah* burns hot and relentless
on peoples pushed to the margins,
exposed, defenseless
        like chaff before a fire.

This modern conflagration is but a recapitulation
of patterns dating back to our country's creation
seen all too clearly in slave ship and plantation,
in sharecropper hut and urban underclass station,
reaching full flower
        in our Black prison nation.

A world apart, so black, so rife with misery,
the prison is utterly foreign to those
who see only the wealthy,
especially the white and wealthy,
those paragons of privilege
given a healthy dose of justice
        in the land of the free.

So it is, as ever, a given:
The rich get richer
and the poor get prison.
Especially in the projects
        where color is life's prism.

A lucky few trapped in prison
come risen (after three decades

not three days) but they, unlike Christ,
are unbidden, unexpected
and unwelcome
     in the land where only

the White
    and Wealthy
        are truly Free.

Note: "Old Hannah" is a name for the sun in slave and plantation prison songs. According to 2017 statistics from the U.S. Bureau of Justice, for every 100,000 residents, 397 white people and 2336 Black people are in prison with a sentence of more than one year — more than five times as many Blacks than whites. The disparity on Death Row is even more extreme.

features from The List: banished, disparity

Lunarspider, Lord of Nothing

by George T. Wilkerson

big and bulky with muscle and bullshit
attitude, 'Cifer likes to spread
his traps in front of men
in here who flit about

their days, complacent. walking laps
all *la-dee-dah*
he'll drop a sandwich baggie full of contraband
((weed, pills, slivers of K-2, bookie tickets))

as bait.   then wait
for an idiot to pick it up to pocket it
or try to be helpful like, "hey, you dropped this,"
and hand it to him. he'll snap WHATTHEFUCK

YOUDOINTOUCHINMYSHIT! or the like
to tangle them in confrontation,
betting he can back them down
with his hard mouth his fists his reputation.

he's gotten knocked out for it
a couple times, yet still, the snares,
'Cifer says he's doing us a service
with lessons meant to enlighten

men to dangers hidden in other prisons
in case we leave Death Row. but i know
a lunatic when i see one. as if
moonstruck, he does this every month

after he gets off his psych meds. i also know
he's wrapped up in his failed attempts:

                    his ex
                    his silly lisp
                    his drug addictions
                    his imminent execution

when it comes to them
he's angry yet broken-
fanged,
impotent
to change
his fates.
his webs are but a poisoned way
to cocoon himself in lies. to convince
himself that he is in control
and unafraid
to die.

features from The List: grief, mental health, mortality

Lightbearers
by Robert Johnson

"You gave me hope," he said, looking hopeful, almost cheerful. "I'd given up, you know, thrown in the towel, said, 'This is it.' And it was. You could say I was ready. I'd accepted it, not that it was easy. But I saw it coming and I was ready to throw myself under the bus. Or stand right out in front of it. And I was numb, just didn't care. Then you gave me hope. Now, right now, I have hope."

I nodded, feeling a little queasy. He nodded, then went on. "You guys care. I feel like I'm alive. The past, well, it just don't hurt as much. Even if I can't forget, I can forgive. Forgive *her*, my mom. She was just a child when she had me, and when she left me in the streets, homeless. Forgive myself, for what I turned out to be. A junkie, mugger, murderer of helpless old women. Well, only one old woman, but she was a grandmother, and her grandchildren were in the car. The car I tried to steal before all hell broke loose, and she was dead and I was dead, or at least sentenced to death. But I'm not done yet. I can still be somebody. I can redeem myself. I have hope."

Sitting on death row, smiling at a man I'd come to know and like, I shared that hope, even reveled in it. At first. Fighting the death penalty — it's the good fight, right? Hopeful. I was hopeful — uneasy, even at the outset, because this is a big deal, but hopeful.

And that hope stayed with me long after that visit. Even as his appeals were denied and his bids for commutation were denied, and even as his requests for extended last visits were denied, I clung to the hope that *he* had hope and that there were grounds for hope.

I see him sometimes, if I let my mind wander: standing in his cell, ten feet from the execution chamber, hopeful for a last-minute visit, maybe even a last-minute reprieve. I see him in my dreams. If I try hard, I see him on the gurney, and with a herculean effort, I cling to the hope that he had hope and there were grounds for hope, right up until the end. Even though it was hopeless, maybe from the start.

features from The List: family, grief, limbo

Part IV:
Exit

Acceptance: Letter to My Mom, 2021
by George T. Wilkerson

Dear Mom,

I can't believe two people in our family would be diagnosed with cancer the same year. First my little brother, now my Mom? I know God knows what He's doing, but it's times like these that make it hard to keep the faith.

What's Albert got — six months? I am grateful they caught yours in time, but I still about fell out. I had to just lock in my cell for several days, get away from everybody. You mentioned that you worried about nobody being there for me, what with Dad dying during my trial, now Albert's on the way, and, one day, you. I feel like all this worrying about me isn't helping you.

So I want to reassure you a little. You know how I work on various writing projects? Often, I work with people on the outside, collaborating with them. I don't know if this is Providence or Fate, but it feels somehow sacred: I met this woman, another writer, and she loves poetry as much as I do — can you believe that? I can't really explain how connected I feel with her; though physically imprisoned still, when we talk on the phone (I'm so glad death row has them now!) it feels like I've come home. I think she's the first real friend I've made in a very long time, and I'm certain she's going to be there for me. Some things you just *know*, right? So don't worry, Mom. I have God and I have my friend. I'm not alone.

I love you, Mom. I'll call next week as usual.

Your son,
George

features from The List: banished, diminished, family, grief, mortality

Lethal Rejection: Reveries and Ruminations on the Edge of Execution

by Robert Johnson

I gaze up at the bright light and feel a stab of pain that reaches deep into my head. I squeeze my eyes shut, then slowly open them, examining the grainy images that float before me as my eyes adjust, feeling better for a moment. I blink a few times, then close my eyes firmly, going inside myself. What a long, strange trip it's been.

I notice a faint hum timed to the flickering of the fluorescent lights above me. My head aches from the constant echo of metal gates lurching open and slamming shut. I imagine the world outside the cocoon of my inert body. I see the floor: gray on gray, concrete with a dull sheen sealed in grime. I see the building: brick, steel, and glass so dirty in places it's permanently stained; the roof crowned by barbed wire; the hard ground a reluctant host to scraggly weeds; a few feral cats out for the hunt; the high wall holding this hard world together, a planet in its own solitary orbit; and me at the center, in the execution chamber.

I breathe deeply. Every muscle in my body unwinds, giving just a little. I feel okay — a little groggy, but okay. My mind drifts, like I'm sedated or just worn out. Hazy images from my past float over me in slow, undulating waves. I revisit scenes from my life, each laced with sadness and loss, but it doesn't bother me. Like it's someone else's life, not mine. I've hurt people, but it seems like ages ago, in another life. People have hurt me. It hardly matters now.

But she matters. I loved her and I hated her. I was glad I killed her, and I sorely miss her. She's grown on me, grown in me, become part of me. She's the background to my miserable existence, lurking in the shadows. On Death Row. In the Death House. Now, on the gurney. Crime and punishment, now and forever, Amen.

I catch a familiar scent from the mess hall, batter hitting grease, and I brighten, shaking off my sadness, feeling warm all over. Pancakes. Home.

Is it morning? I know what awaits me: My mom, bearing eggs and pancakes and sausage, fried up in a heavy cast iron pan, eggs sizzling when they hit the plate, pancakes bubbling with syrup, sausages riding shotgun. My favorite meal, life-sustaining; her favorite meal, home-sustaining. Easy to make and always a big hit.

I open my eyes to get up and stop — I see men staring down at me. One is wearing a white shirt with a black tie and a tiny silver tie clasp shaped like a pair of handcuffs. I marvel at the detail. I wonder if he has an itty-bitty key opening the door to freedom. Or closing it. Who are these men, and how did they get here? They speak among themselves as if I'm not here, not a real person like I am to my mother.

"It's time to eat," Mom says in that sing-song voice she adopts when she has breakfast ready and no lumbering teenager at the table to eat in big gulps.

"I'm starved," I say from under cool sheets tucked tightly around me.

"Of course you are, dear. That's why I made your favorite breakfast."

I nod.

"Just the way you like it, son. Just right. You know how upset you get when things aren't just right."

"Now mom, let's not go there . . ."

"But son, hasn't that been the story of your life? Hurting people you can't control?"

Mom warned me about her. I didn't listen.

"Listen, Mom," I say, firmly but gently, I hope. "I'm not that man anymore."

She nods, murmurs, "Okay." I sense she has her doubts. I can't blame her, but it hurts.

The men are still talking, but I can't make out what they are saying.

My mother approaches the table, pan in hand. I'm sitting at attention with knife and fork. I sit quietly. The pan she carries is as good as a weapon. Not that she'd use it that way, but still, she has a temper. Runs in the family.

Another deep breath. I can almost feel the scent of the pancakes wafting toward me on a cloud of mist: rich in butter, mingled with the aroma of sweet syrup and savory sausage and . . . something sour, something bitter and stale.

My sweat. My own sweat. Jesus, I'm wet and a bit clammy. I smell bad. Did I shower? Did I dry myself before I came to the table?

I look down and see I'm struggling with the pancakes, like they're fighting back, fighting for their lives. The eggs go down like good soldiers, but the pancakes — they're thick and moist and putting up a helluva of a struggle.

"You're mine," I say, almost laughing out loud. "Give it up!"

She wouldn't, not really. Never really loved me. That's why things turned so dark.

The fork slips. I can't hold it still. My hands are sweating. I press harder, and the fork and knife break. I look closely, staring, then I see they are black and plastic and badly mangled.

"Mom," I say, "what's with the plastic?"

"Don't press so hard, dear. You've got to take things in stride."

I couldn't, not with her. I was driven.

"Take it slow, savor it. Eat each meal like it's your last." Zen wisdom from my Irish Catholic mother courtesy of the Great Potato Famine, a staple at our table.

My last real meal was with her, my girl. I thought she was my girl.

But if this is my last meal, shouldn't I eat fast and get more? I mean, this is it, so let's push the envelope till it pushes back and I'm so full I struggle to stay awake, my body hungry for a deep sleep, like I'm drugged, really out like a light.

"You're ready; you can handle this," one of the men states. The words, spoken softly, cascade down from a wide fleshy face, smiling benignly at me from atop a thick neck encased in a tight white collar, emerging from a blue uniform jacket with the name "Capt. Flanagan" etched in bold letters — a genial, decent man, now that I recognize his face.

"You've made the big walk. You're on the gurney, strapped down tight. The needle is in place. No glitches. Relax. The hard stuff is over. You can do this. We're good to go."

Relax? The hard stuff is over? Good to go?

As if reading my mind, Flanagan grimaces, says, "This is hard on everyone."

I look at him blankly. He says, "Sorry, but really, this is a hard job. Nothing personal."

I squint and think carefully, like I'm slow in the head or something, wondering what all this means. This is happening to *me*, right? Not personal?

My girl said as much, when she left me, the night I killed her.

"You put yourself here, really. We're just carrying out the law."

I tried to think clearly. I can only wonder how I put myself on the gurney, strapped down so tightly I can barely move.

Flanagan nods sincerely, like we have an understanding. I see that the men with him have their badges taped to hide their names. The execution team. That's how they roll. Not personal for them. They're strangers

The warden approaches, looking a bit like a funeral director. I recognize him, but his features seem blurry. I squint, and my eyes water.

"The warden has something to read to you, son," says Captain Flanagan.

I'm older than the warden and Flanagan both — I've been here forever; I'm the oldest man in the room, on the row, even. Still, it's comforting to be called "son."

The warden coughs, clears his throat.

"By order of the court . . ." he starts, almost shouting, then trails off. "Hereby . . . whereupon . . . on the appointed date . . . in accordance with . . ." The words run on and run together.

Flanagan leans in, putting his hand on my shoulder, softly. I pull back as much as the straps allow. The needle stings when I move. I lay still, breathing slowly. No one has touched me with gentleness in years. Decades.

"Did you want a few words with the prison chaplain?"

I shake my head no. A conversation is more than I can manage. It's hard to think. The clanging doors and humming lights make my head hurt like hell. My forehead is damp; my eyes itch.

"Let's go. Let's do it, Captain." I wonder at my own words: confident, like I've got things under control.

"Any last words?"

"I'm sorry. Really sorry." And I am, for so many things, but it's all so complicated and I can't think clearly to say more.

The Beatles' song, our song, starts to play in my head: "All You Need is Love." Over and over, like a lullaby. We loved that song. Until we didn't love each other. Or at least she didn't love me.

"Ready?" says the warden.

I nod.

"Are you *really* ready, Christopher?"

Christopher!

I open my eyes wide, now sensing the danger around me. When Mom calls me Christopher, I know I'm in trouble.

I go to say, "Yeah, I'm fine, full and fine with a solid breakfast under my belt, ready for the day, ready to roll . . ." but I can't get the words out. My throat is on fire, burning like a forest blaze. I feel like I'm choking, choking on a big-ass chunk of soggy pancake, thick as paste, and my throat is filling up and I can't swallow. I gag, gasping, struggling to get air. I feel crazy panic well up in my chest, and my chest is filling up like a goddamn balloon about to burst and my heart, it's squeezed tight but banging away like a jackhammer — *boom baboom, boom baboom* — and my arms are getting heavy, like lead, like they're holding up the

88

whole damn world, and I feel a surge of heat, like I'm burning up inside.

"Mom, I made a real mess and I'm scared and . . ."

"Yes, son. You stabbed her so hard you broke . . ."

"Mom, please."

"She was too much for you, wasn't she? You bit off more than you could chew, didn't you? I told you . . ."

Everyone is looking at me. I can see their silhouettes against the bright lights; they are studying me like a specimen, some sort of exotic creature, fresh from the wild. .

I stare back, my eyes open wide, pushing out like they're about to blow up, like frogs' eyes ready to burst.

Help me! I'm dying, right here in front of you! Somebody do something! Did she scream the same words, in her head, at the end? Crime and punishment, now and forever, Amen.

The men start to retreat, fade away. Their faces grow softer; the light dims. My mood calms, like this is all fine with me, life in gray, life fading away, life floating on air, lifting me off the ground, my body drifting into space — a sweet darkness wrapping me in a soft, moist blanket, damp with sweat but warm, warm like the dull light that slowly, almost tenderly, envelopes me . . .

features from The List: diminished, displayed, family, mortality, staff

A Single Olive

by Sarah Bousquet

A single olive
Unpitted
Black against the
Bright white plate

The guard who brought it to her
Could not help
But ask
Why

She smiled,
A pained smile
Corrupted
By the horrors of prison

She said
My mother used to say
If you ate
An unpitted olive,
An olive tree
Would grow
In your stomach

She said
Someone once told me
Olive trees
Mean peace

She said
Maybe, just maybe
If I eat this
An olive tree will grow
From my grave

And finally bring me peace

features from The List: family, grief, mortality, staff

Empty (2019) by Benjamin Feder

Bone Orchard
by George T. Wilkerson

everything about James is dramatic.
one of those guys who's gone
through fire, soul burned to bone,
leaving behind a scorched, skeletonized intensity.

eyes like cigarette holes burnt into a blanket.
to hear James talk, voice grained in static,
is to witness arrogance manifest:
standing tall at five-five, bald, old

skinhead battered with scars, he thrusts his chest
— always ready for a fight —
and all he says:
"i know how to do *time.*"

he'd done a life
sentence before catching his death.
when i ask him about the differences
he says, "well . . . the biggest thing is calendars.

notice you don't see many around here? on the yard
everybody's watching their calendar,
scratching off days. it's counting down —
every day's closer to home.

you know?
in *here,* it's just counting down.
but it don't bother
me: i'm ready for this muthafucka

to end!"

———————

93

genius loci: 1) guardian of a place.
2) the spirit of a place,
the character or atmosphere of it —
the impression it makes on the mind.

let's see . . . death guards this place.
death is the spirit of this place;
its character or atmosphere is death —
death is the impression it makes

on the mind: death
                   death
                   death
                   death

——————

on the yard: for us
it means a release
date. it suggests outside
even though you're still inside.

it means looking forward
to something
rather than backward
at something.

——————

perhaps another language
can say it best, with flourish,
like those flower-patterned skulls
for *día de los muertos* —

the day of the dead.
a way to celebrate death
as a way to highlight
life.

——————

though no less arrogant and dramatic,
the fire turned Jeff to ash. sixty-ish,
he's like a certified ghost, damned
skin so white he couldn't tan

at gunpoint. anger and sadness
have crystallized his face,
his features rigormortised with them.
even when present

time slides by on grease,
slips, falls painfully into past:
every conversation is a chance
to tell and retell the same stories.

incidents have turned into anecdotes.
anecdotes turn imperfect memories from forty
years ago, when free, into absolute certainties.
how often i've noticed

slight modifications, upgrades, clever cuts.
the longer time
stretches the fewer of us left
to remind him that his life is not his life

now — it's the epic legend
he tells to others,
sure,
but mainly to himself.

———————

a *memento mori* is a reduction of something
significant — such as a man — into something
irreparably diminished. literally: "remember that you must
    die."
usually it's an object, like that decorative skull, a reminder

of death or mortality. in here,
red-painted surfaces everywhere —
red doors and jambs, sills and shelves,
red jumpsuits —

or when we asked
our overseers for GED classes,
their response: "You are *not*
here to be rehabilitated."

somehow,
strangely,
i forget
i am here

to die.

*features from The List: calendars, grief, idle, limbo, masks,
mortality, staff*

Coldest
by Robert Johnson

I can take or leave executions.
It's not a job I like or dislike.
It's a job I've been asked to do.
I try to go about every job
in the most professional manner I can.
If we had ten executions tomorrow,
it wouldn't bother me. I would
condition my mind to get me through it.

Note: These are the words of an Execution Team Officer.

features from The List: staff

Burnt Offerings
by Robert Johnson

there
in the damp basement
of the aging prison
near the
chair

death
the scent
of burnt offerings
hangs heavy
in the air

a
devil's brew
of mildew, sweat
and raw
fear

the chair
is gone

it's the needle now

the smell
lives on

Note: While different states use various methods of execution, each death chamber emits a psychic "smell." Even when or if executions stop, the chamber draws the minds of prisoners.

features from The List: mortality

Six Feet
by George T. Wilkerson

my self-isolating
family no longer visits me. we must keep everyone
at arm's length ------ flatten the curve
of yearning for connection. we must strap on masks

before exiting our cells; many of us shelter in place
instead, to be authentic. we recoil when people
within striking distance move too quickly
in our direction, or cough or sneeze. the consequences

of injury or sickness is a constant
topic base-coded into our reflexes.
everybody knows the terms
medical and *attention* merely cohabit

our sentences on death row
like a loveless marriage. we stockpile
ramen, batteries, coffee, toiletries, and stamps as money
from family dries up. i could last perhaps

two months. letters take longer
and longer to reach us. weeks, sometimes
months. if pressed, most of us would admit to feeling
abandoned or forgotten, in need

of a hug. the sturdy kind, where you can't breathe. still
we check the news each day, praying
not to recognize the names
of people beaten over toilet paper.

AND THEN THE PANDEMIC BEGAN
and the prison issued restrictions, first

prohibiting all visitors, preachers, teachers. now
my family can't visit even if they tried. the prison

distributed masks, flimsy black
fabric behind which we can relax

the veneers of indifference we'd kept flexed
on our faces. guards posted memos to warn us

that if we break the coronavirus
restrictions again, they will punish us —

for real this time —
and medical staff taped glossy,

cartoonish diagrams every-fucking-where: on the pods,
up and down the hallway walls like family photos,

cheerfully reminding us that
to get too close to anyone now is to risk

one's life. the monetary fines, weeks in the hole,
and death for disobedience — these toothless threats

are just for show, for public health
inspectors, for prison administrators to claim they *tried*

to keep us from dying before our scheduled execution.
it's been eighteen months since the pandemic

restrictions began and nobody here's gone to lock-up
despite our blatant violations. in fact, we're trapped

on our blocks: no church, no classes. familiarity breeds
contempt, some say. so, in a way, the prison *is*

enforcing social isolation. the childish medical diagrams
depict two featureless blue-gray humanoids and i

100

can't tell which way their blank faces face, though
their bodies point forward, toward me. a bright red arrow

spreads their anonymous bodies apart, with SIX FEET
written incandescently above them, like divine knowledge

dropped. i imagine that
it'd be more impactful to translate the isolation image

into two *real* people who stand facing one another
like lovers, or perhaps friends or brothers,

father and son. better yet my mom and me,
our arms stretching toward each other —

hers smooth and tan, mine sleeved in black tattoos —
but our hug cannot penetrate the Plexiglas between us.

that's six feet.
the right distance

is as long as the grave is deep.

*features from The List: banished, family, idle, masks,
mortality, staff*

Transubstantiation
by Robert Johnson

Changing

    people into felons
    felons into objects
    objects into grist

for the Death House

features from The List: mortality

Afterword
The Afterlife of Executions
by Robert Johnson

There was death and ghosts everywhere. The row was haunted by the men who died in the electric chair.
   – Anthony Hinton, author, former death row prisoner, Alabama

Our memories of the dead become death row lore, significant to us, living on in our hearts and minds and dreams. We live together, die together, mourn together, and remember.
   – Lyle C. May, author, death row prisoner, North Carolina

I see a man, vaguely familiar, strapped to a chair
an electric chair
which I take in stride —
a statement about my life as a researcher

It dawns on me that this is the man whose execution I
      observed
a few days after the birth of one of my sons

I didn't know him or speak to him

I watched
He watched

Things followed a rigid routine
ending in the morgue

Now this man is waving his hands at me (straps be damned)
asking for help (leather facemask notwithstanding)

Help

Asking me

I wake up

"Save me, Joe Louis, save me," said one poor man
years ago in the Jim Crow South, strapped
in a wooden chair in North Carolina's gas chamber
praying to the iconic boxer of the twentieth century,
a man as famous as Muhammad Ali but no help here

The story, I've learned, is apocryphal but plausible

Pictures of Louis adorned death row cells and gave peace to
    many

Help me this man asks

I didn't then and I don't now
I just watch
That night and then for many nights thereafter

And any night, now and again
Like it or not

I don't

Another night, another man
a man I knew well
strapped to a gurney
head tilted toward me
eyes on me
a look I can't quite read

I gaze back, mute

We'd shared laughs now and again

He'd told me funny stories —
dark, but funny —
one about a bunkie
        (his term for cellmate)
who cleaned their cell day and night
            floor – walls – ceiling
made art out of cigarette wrappers
even furniture:
a dresser, with shelves,
working shelves

Out of cigarette wrappers

"That's when I knew I had to kill him," my friend said

We both laughed —
a moment of bonding

"The Odd Couple on steroids," I said,
referring to a once-famous movie then TV show
about wildly mismatched roommates
to let him know I'd listened with care

He'd never heard of The Odd Couple

So there were barriers between us

I would have so much liked a word with him at the end
but there are no happy endings in the Death House

    even in dreams

Appendix: The List

Synthesized answers, in alphabetical order, in response to this question: *What makes serving time under a death sentence distinct from serving time with a release date?*

Attachments: Many on Death Row hold this attitude: "This is all I have left . . ." They cling to TV, commissary items, phone calls, recreation, terrified of losing the few creature comforts they have — especially by spending their last days in solitary confinement, aka the hole.

Banished: Between physical segregation, even from other prisoners, and the mainstream stereotype about Death Row prisoners, we feel forsaken, abandoned, forgotten, demonized as "the worst of the worst." About one in ten prisoners are actually innocent, and historically, five of seven people who initially receive a death sentence ultimately either get out of prison or get a sentence reduction on appeal. The damage, however, is permanent.

Calendars: On New Year's Eve, guys in Regular Population with a release date might smash things, kick on doors, and get drunk to celebrate another year closer to home. On Death Row, though, many avoid tracking time with calendars. Our perception of time itself warps: years pass fast as weeks yet somehow feel like eternity. Some holidays, though, mark the passage of time.

Diminished: We're here so long, people we love who live on the outside die off one by one. Even among us, guys die or get executed. Having spent decades together on a pod, or perhaps the cell next door, we find the losses to be traumatic.

Disparity: On Death Row, the socioeconomic disparity between who gets sentenced and who doesn't is even more stark than in Regular Population. Death Row consists predominantly of people of Color — all poor. No wealthy people here.

Displayed: Tour groups come through regularly to view us through Plexiglas.

Family: Our loved ones must wrestle with our reality. To many, it's easiest to reckon us as dead already and to treat us so. Those who don't, who stay in contact, do our time with us.

Grief: Many guys on Death Row grieve nonstop — some for victims of their crimes, some for themselves (anticipatory grief), dwelling on all they've lost. Grief is often characterized as having five distinct stages. Using this model, many here get stuck in various stages:

Denial – false hopes for release

Anger – recriminations, blame, etc.

Bargaining – e.g., *I would sell my soul to the Devil to get off Death Row.*

Depression – ruminating on one's fate; remorse/repentance

Acceptance – This is rare.

Groundhog Day: By not having access to a range of activities, unlike guys in Regular Population, Death Row feels like a sensory deprivation chamber where the same day plays on a loop, just like in the movie *Groundhog Day.*

Idle: We're offered few to no activities, programs, classes, etc.

Limbo: Because capital cases usually take decades (some guys have been here thirty to forty years) to crawl through appellate courts before a final decision is rendered, we often feel like our lives are in a state of suspended animation between life and death, hope and despair. The latest innocent, Henry McCollum, spent thirty-one years here on North Carolina's Death Row before being exonerated.

110

<u>Masks</u>: Most struggle with utter despair yet try to hide it behind a metaphorical mask. Nevertheless, it lurks in the eyes and influences behavior in clear ways.

<u>Mental Health</u>: About half of our population has been diagnosed with serious and/or persistent mental disorders. Many take prescription psych meds. Sometimes, Med Call draws more people than Chow Call.

<u>Mortality</u>: This is the most distinct feature. We are constantly confronted by the reality that we are here to die. We may try to ignore it, but reminders are everywhere, in many forms, such as our red jumpsuits.

<u>Segregation</u>: Death Row prisoners are kept completely isolated from Regular Population. Whenever a Death Row prisoner moves through the prison, such as to see a loved one in a visitation booth, they cannot in any way interact with guys in Regular Population.

<u>Staff</u>: All staff and volunteers — whether guards, nurses, teachers, etc. — must make a choice regarding their own humanity and ours, which determines how they treat us: hard or with compassion. No one is unaffected by this place.

<u>Static</u>: Unlike Regular Population, Death Row's turnover rate is low and slow. Being cooped up with the same faces for so long, we really come to know each other, which makes executions that much harder.

Appendix: Thematic Index

Attachments
   Any Day Now
   A Body is a Home
   The Code
   Fat Brown Quarters

Banished
   Acceptance: Letter to My Mom, 2021
   Black Prison Nation
   The Code
   The Huggy Boys: Letter to My Mom, 2011
   The Infiltrator
   Keep It Moving
   The Knowledge of Good and Evil
   Lights Out
   Little Sister
   Pod People
   Pretending to be Human
   Six Feet
   Welcome: Letter to My Mom, 2006
   Witness

Calendars
   Bone Orchard
   Clorox
   Fat Brown Quarters
   Flesh is Weak
   The Knowledge of Good and Evil

Diminished
   Acceptance: Letter to My Mom, 2021
   Any Day Now
   Keep It Moving
   Lethal Rejection

Talking to My Mom in Autumn, 2016

Disparity
  Black Prison Nation
  The Code

Displayed
  Lethal Rejection
  Pretending to be Human

Family
  Acceptance: Letter to My Mom, 2021
  A Body is a Home
  Clorox
  Lethal Rejection
  Lightbearers
  Little Sister
  A Single Olive
  Six Feet
  Talking to My Mom in Autumn, 2016
  Witness

Grief
  Acceptance: Letter to My Mom, 2021
  Bone Orchard
  Clorox
  Keep It Moving
  The Knowledge of Good and Evil
  Last Night Lullaby
  Lightbearers
  Lights Out
  Little Sister
  Lunarspider, Lord of Nothing
  Pod People
  A Single Olive
  Snakes and Thunder
  Talking to My Mom in Autumn, 2016

Groundhog Day
    Circadian Rhythm
    The Code
    Pod People

Idle
    Bone Orchard
    Fat Brown Quarters
    The Huggy Boys: Letter to My Mom, 2011
    Six Feet
    Snakes and Thunder

Limbo
    Bone Orchard
    Circadian Rhythm
    The Death House is No House
    Flesh is Weak
    Lightbearers
    Lights Out

Masks
    Bone Orchard
    The Huggy Boys: Letter to My Mom, 2011
    Keep It Moving
    Six Feet

Mental Health
    Any Day Now
    Keep It Moving
    Lunarspider: Lord of Nothing
    Pod People
    Snakes and Thunder

Mortality
    Acceptance: Letter to My Mom, 2021
    Any Day Now
    A Body is a Home
    Bone Orchard

Burnt Offerings
Circadian Rhythm
The Death House is No House
Fat Brown Quarters
Flesh is Weak
Keep It Moving
Last Night Lullaby
Lethal Rejection
Lunarspider, Lord of Nothing
A Single Olive
Six Feet
Transubstantiation
Welcome: Letter to My Mom, 2006

Segregation
The Huggy Boys: Letter to My Mom, 2011
Lights Out
Welcome: Letter to My Mom, 2006

Staff
A Body is a Home
Bone Orchard
The Code
Coldest
The Infiltrator
Keep It Moving
The Knowledge of Good and Evil
Lethal Rejection
A Single Olive
Six Feet
Snakes and Thunder
Welcome: Letter to My Mom, 2006
Witness

Static
The Huggy Boys: Letter to My Mom, 2011
Keep It Moving
Snakes and Thunder

116

About the Authors & Contributors

George T. Wilkerson is a self-taught, award-winning poet, writer, and artist incarcerated on North Carolina's Death Row. His poetry has appeared in *Poetry*, *Bayou Magazine*, *Prime Number Magazine*, and elsewhere. His essays and stories have appeared in *The Marshall Project*, the PEN anthology *The Named and the Nameless*, the anthology *Right Here, Right Now*, and elsewhere. He has won four PEN awards, is a coauthor of *Crimson Letters: Voices from Death Row*, has edited the anthology *You'll Be Smarter than Us*, and is editor of *Compassion*, a newsletter by and for Death Row prisoners in America. His poetry collection *Interface*, about his childhood in the projects and life on Death Row, won the 2022 Victor Hassine Memorial Scholarship. During the one hour a day George isn't patting himself on the back for all of his accomplishments, he is vigorously training to win the award for World's Humblest Person. To read more of George's writing, visit katbodrie.com/georgewilkerson.

Robert Johnson is a professor of Justice, Law, and Criminology at American University; editor and publisher of BleakHouse Publishing; and an award-winning author of books and articles on crime and punishment, including works of social science, law, poetry, and fiction. He has testified or provided expert affidavits in capital and other criminal cases in many venues, including U.S. state and federal courts, the U.S. Congress, and the European Commission of Human Rights. He is best known for his books on prison life and the death penalty: *Hard Time: Understanding and Reforming the Prison, Condemned to Die: Life Under Sentence of Death*, and *Death Work: A Study of the Modern Execution Process,* which received the Outstanding Book Award of the Academy of Criminal Justice Sciences. Johnson is a Distinguished Alumnus of the School of Criminal Justice, Nelson A. Rockefeller College of Public

Affairs and Policy at the University at Albany, State University of New York.

Sarah Bousquet is a graduate student at the University of Pennsylvania's School of Social Policy and Practice. She is studying for dual master's degrees in Social Work and Social Policy. She is passionate about working with sexual violence survivors and their intersection with the juvenile legal system. Her poem "A Single Olive" appears on page 90.

Benjamin Feder is an honors graduate of American University, holding Bachelor of Arts and Master of Arts degrees in Art History with a focus on humanism and the Italian Renaissance. His experiences as both an artist and a student of art history are what initially compelled him to start a career in the art industry. Benjamin has worked in museums and galleries in both New York City and Washington, D.C., and is currently working at one of D.C.'s top art advisory firms. As an artist, Benjamin's favorite medium is clay, though he often includes mixed media into his sculptures. A picture of his sculpture "Empty" appears on page 92.

About the Artists, Editors, & Designers

Kat Bodrie is a professional writer and editor based in Winston-Salem, North Carolina. Her editorial credits include *Crimson Letters: Voices from Death Row* (second edition), *1808: Greensboro's Monthly*, and *Winston-Salem Monthly*. A recovering community college instructor, she writes about the intersection between sexuality and spirituality. Her poetry has appeared in *North Meridian Review, Poetry South, West Texas Literary Review*, and elsewhere. Read her writing and seek her services at katbodrie.com.

Casey Chiappetta is an American University alumna who received her Master of Science in Justice, Law, and Criminology in 2019 and her Bachelor of Arts in Sociology in 2017. She is the recipient of the outstanding scholarship award at both the undergraduate and graduate levels, the first person to receive both prestigious awards. Casey currently works with The Pew Charitable Trusts. At Pew, she conducts research and manages research grants focused on making the civil legal system more equitable, open, and efficient. Prior, she worked at the National Legal Aid and Defender Association, providing technical assistance to civil legal aid and leading research on online dispute resolution. Her work has been published in *Disability & Society, Family Court Review*, and *MIE Journal*, among others.

Charlotte Lopez-Jauffret is pursuing a doctoral degree in Justice, Law, and Criminology from American University. While obtaining her Master of Forensic Science at George Washington University, she worked as a DNA technician at a private lab and later as a Forensic Intelligence Analyst in the public sector. Currently, she is interested in various topics such as the standards of evidence, the digestion of forensic science by laypersons, and sexual assault litigation.

Donald Kinney has photographed in and around Marin County, California, taking a particular interest in wildlife and landscapes. View his other work at donaldkinney.com.

Sophia Auger Madden is an American University alumna who has a Bachelor of Arts in Justice, Law, and Criminology. She is currently pursuing a Certificate in Editing from the University of Chicago's Graham School. By combining her academic background with a passion for reading, Sophia hopes to use editing as a tool to facilitate the sharing of ideas and storytelling.

Other Titles from BleakHouse Publishing

Interface, George T. Wilkerson

Crass Casualties, Anthony G. Amsterdam

Behind These Fences, E.L.

Pagan, John Corley

Silent, We Sit, Emily Dalgo

Black Bone: Poems on Crime and Punishment, Race and Justice, Alexa Marie Kelly

An Elegy for Old Terrors, Zoé Orfanos

Up the River, Chandra Bozelko

Distant Thunder, Charles Huckelbury

Enclosures: Reflections from the Prison Cell and the Hospital Bed, Shirin Karimi

A Zoo Near You, Robert Johnson et al.

Origami Heart: Poems by a Woman Doing Life, Erin George

Tales from the Purple Penguin, Charles Huckelbury

Burnt Offerings, Robert Johnson

CPSIA information can be obtained
at www.ICGtesting.com
Printed in the USA
BVHW032226220922
647830BV00012B/136